Confessions of a Word Lush

Confessions of a Word Lush

Tales of lexical excess

by

James Harbeck

ISBN 978-1-387-74439-8

www.lulu.com

Contents

I dedicate this book to Aina, who keeps me happy,
and to all the readers of Sesquiotica, who keep me writing.

frosh

AH, I REMEMBER FROSH WEEK. Well, actually, I don't really, not my own, anyway; as the actress said to the archbishop – or was it the converse? – it was long ago, and I was drunk. With excitement, I mean, of course. But, ah, to see those lively young faces about to embark on what they mistakenly believe is the beginning of adulthood (no, sweeties, not yet, but you do get to pretend and rehearse) – a step up from high school, at that fountain of knowledge where they will gather to drink (ever wonder how many campus bars are called the Pierian Spring? not enough, probably). So I gladly man the Order of Logogustation table at the local university's frosh week, even though visitors often include (a) speckly social maladepts in whom I uncomfortably recognize an earlier version of myself and (b) entirely typical youth for whom excessive intellectual exercise is likely to elicit blank looks usually gotten from unexceptional canines being addressed in monotonous Esperanto.

Today I was visited by a tidy pair of the latter sort whom I, in a moment of hope, invited to taste the word *frosh*.

"Frash?" said the female of the pair. "Oh my gad, is this like some kind of tast?"

"Just say it a few times and say what it feels like to say it."

"Frash... frash, frash, frash. It's like, fresh. Fraaaaaaash."

"That's cuz it's from 'fresh,'" her male cohort pointed out. "Like, it's so obvious: freshman – frosh."

"Well, yeah, OK, I knew that?"

"But why?" I asked. "Why go from *fresh* to *frosh*? Do we go from *mesh* to *mosh*?"

"Mosh pit!" the guy replied. "Yeah, like mesh pit, but mosh!"

"Except that comes from *mash*," I said.

"Omigad, how d'you know this stuff?" the girl drawled.

1

I tapped a few keystrokes into my laptop. "The *Oxford English Dictionary* tells me that *frosh* has been short for *freshman* since at least 1915, and it may have gone from *fresh* to *frosh* under the influence of the German word *Frosch*, meaning 'frog,' which was also used in some places to refer to elementary-school kids."

The guy crossed his arms. "So, like, you're saying we're German frogs."

"At a glance," I replied, "I don't think so. Though you might be a bit green around the gills after too many Jäger bombs this weekend."

"Frags don't have gells," the girl pointed out. "They're amphebians."

"True enough," I said. "But anyway, nobody thinks of frogs now when someone says *frosh*, right?"

"Like, more likely fesh?"

"Fish?" the guy said. "Frosh – fish? Frosh – *wash*, I think."

"Cuz, like, you don't?"

"Sure," I said, "the sound of *frosh* is sort of like the sound of a washing machine, 'frosh-frosh frosh-frosh frosh-frosh.' Then they tumble you, put you through the wringer, and you come out clean."

"Clean is so nat what frash makes me think. So far."

"How 'bout, like," the guy made a bit of head bobbling as he spoke, "*frosh*-tration?" He made a sideways glance at the girl.

A relevant pun. I was a bit impressed.

"Oh that's like, so funny? or not?" the girl said.

"It could also be a dog kind of sound," I offered, and made fat hound sort of noise: "Frosh! Frosh!"

"Dude, OK" – the guy swept his hand to half-pointing – "you know what that really sounds like?" He mimed an act of emesis over an imaginary toilet bowl: "Frosh!"

"Omigad," the girl said, very equivocally, "that's so perfact."

loom

DARYL, MARGOT, AND I were sitting by food court windows overlooking Yonge Street, observing the ebb and – mostly – flow of life below, and the conversation meandered into politics.

"In loom of a fall election," Daryl said, "I –"

"Wait," Margot cut him off. "In what?"

"In loom of a fall election."

"You mean *in lieu*," she said, her index finger admonitory.

"I sure don't," Daryl said. "*In lieu* means 'in place of.' I'm not talking about that. There's a fall election coming, it's looming in the near future, and we're in the loom of it. It's looming over us."

"You can't say that!" Margot protested.

"I think he just did," I said. "But I haven't heard it before."

"Look," Daryl said, "it gets used. Google it, you'll find enough hits. Anyway, as it happens, I just saw it used in the news headline on that TV screen." He pointed at one of the coven of screens stationed throughout the food court showing news and advertising. "If journalists are using it, it's in use."

Margot gave a little shudder. Her disaffection for the English of journalists was not a secret to those who knew her. "But what is a *loom*?" she said with asperity. "I mean, a device for weaving…"

"Originally a tool of any kind," I said. "A good old Anglo-Saxon word, over the centuries narrowed in meaning."

"A political machine," Daryl said. "Not what I had in mind, though. *Loom* is the looming shape, looming presence. I looked it up. Something seen at first indistinctly, as, for instance, a ship on the horizon, is a loom."

"But we're not *in* it." Margot jabbed her finger into her coffee cup, making a small splash. She sucked the coffee off her fingertip and added, "I think you're a loon."

"*Loom*'s a word for that, too," Daryl said. "A kind of loon – or its meat, for cooking – is sometimes called *loom*. Actually, *loon* comes from *loom*, not the other way around. Of course the etymology of this *loom* is different."

"Well," I said, "a fall election will eat up plenty of loonies, we can be sure."

"And," Daryl continued, "the etymology of *loom*, the verb, is different from that of *loom*, the implement, thought they're both Germanic. But there's a fair bit about the verb that's obscured in the mists of time."

"Looming, as it were," I said.

Margot riposted. "I think you just grabbed this word, *loom*, because it has an echo of *doom* and other shadowy suggestions from that spooky *oo*, and this vague image of something overbearing in the fog, and you stuffed it into the form of an existing phrase in place of the *lieu*." ("Not in place of the *loo*!" Daryl protested, crossing his legs as though interdicted from micturition.) "I find that a bit malapropriate," she concluded.

"Can you say *malapropriate*?" I exclaimed. Daryl, meanwhile, was making spooky gestures with his hands and leaning forward saying "Loom! Loooooom! Lllllloooooommmmm!"

"I just did," Margot said to me, folding her arms. "So there. *Malaprop* plus *inappropriate*. Two can play." (In fact, a bit of checking later showed that *malappropriate* exists as a synonym for *inappropriate*. Alas, there goes that bit of fun.) "Oh, knock that off," she snapped at Daryl, "you sound like a sick cow."

"Sheep would be more appropriate for an election," I said. "Like lambs to the slaughter."

"*Looms* to the slaughter!" Daryl said, clearly having a bit too much fun.

"Well, I don't like this new phrase, *in loom of*," Margot declared, in case we had missed the fact. "It's bound to cause confusion, and it simply sounds ill-educated."

"And you would use what in its place?" Daryl demanded.

4

"In the… in advance of… ahead of…" Margot winced; she knew that she had just uttered a bit of journalese: *Ahead of a fall election, X is doing Y.* "Um, *With a fall election looming…*"

"I like *in loom of* better," Daryl declared. "And so do they." He gestured at the TV. "It's catching on."

"Well, it's appropriate for politics, anyway," I said. "It may not be an heirloom, but it's a hot air loom."

"What a tangled web we weave when first we practice to deceive!" Daryl added.

"Such is the fruit of the loom," Margot muttered, gazing into her near-empty coffee cup.

dioecious

I WAS HAVING A SESSION with that noted word-tasting couple Edgar Frick and Marilyn Frack, well known for showing up at logogustations in matching black leather. We turned to the books and were served up *diœcious*.

"Die-o-ee-shus," Marilyn said.

"No, dear, that's a ligature. A digraph. Die-ee-shus," Edgar replied, rolling the word around in his mouth, starting wide open and easing down into a closing pair of dewy voiceless fricatives.

"A ligature," Marilyn said, glancing at her wrists. "Digamous? Mmm. Delicious."

"One would think it might be spelled like *diet* with an *i-o-u-s*," Edgar mused, omphaloskeptic (to the extent to which his omphalos was skeptible, his figure more global with each year).

"I think," I pointed out with a glance at my etymological dictionary, "that digamous might be on the mark, given that it was first with the Greeks and then with the Romans."

"And now we get to party with it," Marilyn chirped, an had another sip of it: "*Diœcious*. How edacious."

"Well, I rather think it is the spice of life," Edgar said. "*Vive la différance.*"

"Oh, back off with the Derrida," I said. "Well –" I turned to Marilyn – "this ten-dollar word really is a two-bit word: your bit and his bit."

"Hmm. I'll bite," she replied. "It sounds sexy, yes?"

"Characterized by two sexes in separate individuals," Edgar explained. "Like certain kinds of flowers. The ones that need bees."

"Or birds." Marilyn leaned forward, creaking her leather.

"Or people," I said. "And, as I adumbrated, the Latin *œc* comes from the Greek *oik* as in *oikos*. The literal sense: having two houses. In this case, one for each sex."

Marilyn was now on Edgar's lap. "We have two houses," she purred in his ear.

"Sex in one and sex in the other," he half-snickered.

I nearly sprained my eyes rolling them. "A plague on both your houses," I said, and headed back to the stacks.

Worcestershire

I was in Boston for a word tasting event, and at the banquet I happened to find myself seated across from Jenna – a student from Tufts University – and her boyfriend, a "townie" from Medford, whose name I at first heard as *Mack* but realized on speaking further with him was *Mark*. Which should tell you a little something about his accent.

The table was well supplied with condiments. Mark reached for one bottle of dark liquid and said, "Wha's dis heah sauce?"

"That's right," I said.

"What?"

"Worcestershire sauce, just like you said."

"Wh—" he turned the bottle and saw the label. "Oh, hey, like the town here in Mass. Wista."

"Yeah, exactly the same. It's named after a county in England – Worcestershire – which is named after the town that the city here in Massachusetts is named after. Only in England they say 'Wooster' rather than 'Wister.'"

"I always sawta wondahed wheah that came from."

"Yeah, originally from the name of a tribe that lived there – back when the Anglo-Saxons had tribes – called the *Wigoran* and from Old English *ceaster*, meaning 'town,' which in turn comes from Latin *castra*, meaning 'fort' or 'camp.'" I pronounced *ceaster* in the Old English way, rather like "chester." "So the town may have grown," I observed, "but the name keeps shrinking."

"I'll say," Jenna said. "My student loan forms have return envelopes addressed to WORC MA. Double-you oh ar see. That's down to four letters."

"Well, dat's cuz yah gonna write a letta home sayin', 'I'm gonna have to *work, ma*, to pay this off.'" I began to see what Jenna liked about Mark. "Anyway," he said, flipping the top open to sniff it, "I hope this sauce ain't the *worst for sure.*" Jenna smiled. Hey! How come *this* guy found a girl who likes puns? When I was his age such girls didn't exist.

He looked at the bottle again. "Hey, this's got a spellin' erra on it."

"Naw," I said. It was a bottle of Lea & Perrins. What were the odds of their misprinting their label?

"Yeah, it's missin' the H. Waw-*chesta.*"

"There isn't an H," I said. "No H after the C."

"Oh, it's spelled differently in England?"

"No, there's no H in the town here in Massachusetts, either. I know everyone says there is, but there's not. It's on the maps and the street signs – where they get past the first four letters. No H."

"Naw, yaw full of it. I grown up heah."

"There are people who've grown up in Toronto who think *Eglinton* is spelled *Eglington,*" I said. "There's no H."

"But you said 'chesta'! So you know theah's an H!" he exclaimed.

"In Old English they spelled that just with a C before the E," I said. "Though in the name of the town Chester in England, they did add the H."

"Look," said Mark, not smiling, "everyone knows: you say it 'Wista,' you spell it 'Waw-chesta.'"

"I know. But they should say you spell it like 'Wor-*sester,*'" I replied.

I glanced at Jenna. I could see that she knew I was right, but she wasn't going to say so. Her lips were pursed to keep it from getting out. She decided to try a diversion. "Can I see the bottle?" She reached for it abruptly, but Mark wasn't quite ready to let go of it. The resulting jerk sent a spurt of sauce across the table and onto my upper torso.

Mark laughed. "Theah, that's proof!" he said. "You *wore* it on yaw *chest* an' *shirt!*"

whilom

"ANYWAYS," SAID JESS, "HE——"

"Oh, please," Margot interrupted, wincing and setting down her cup. "*Please* don't say *anyways*. *Any* goes with the singular. *Any way*."

I looked at Margot as though she had just denied the law of gravity. "It's not a *plural*," I informed her. "It's a genitive. The genitive as an active inflection survives now almost exclusively as the possessive, which has in recent centuries had an unetymological apostrophe inserted, but you see it surviving in forms such as names like *Johns* and *Williams* and in words such as *anyways* – meaning 'of, or by, any way.' The loss of the *s* is due to the same reanalysis you're making, which is not new but is not historical."

"Well, *I* don't like it," Margot declared. Other people in the coffee shop peered over their papers to see if there was some conflict that might prove entertaining. "We don't form new words that way, so to heck with the old ones that use that."

"So you'll be chucking out *woe is me* too?" I said, arching eyebrow and relaxing back.

"That doesn't have any genitive on it!" Margot protested.

"No," said I, "it's a retention of the whilom dative. 'Woe is to me.'"

"*Whilom!*" Jess said. "I love that word. And I love that you said 'whilom dative.'" She leaned forward and clapped her hands together. "Guess why."

I paused for just a moment, then smiled. "Because *whilom* is dative."

"Yes!" she said gleefully.

"You mean you date yourself by using it," Margot said drily, then moistened with some coffee. Everyone else in the joint, sniffing the general topic, had gone back into hiding.

"That would be solipsistic," Jess replied, and turned back to me. "Dative plural."

"Right, of course, the most consistent case ending in Old English: -*um*." Just to prove I was capable of even greater pretentiousness, I started in on Beowulf: "Hwæt! We Gardena in geardagum…"

"Not *hwæt*," Jess riposted, "*hwile*. Um."

"It sounds more *ho-hum* to me," Margot interjected.

"Now, don't talk *whilom* speaking," Jess said, smirking. Score one for the Jess. "*A while* is a time, and *whilom* – from *hwilum* – is 'at times.'"

"But now it really means 'at past times' or 'at a past time,'" I added.

"But why not just use *erstwhile?*" Margot protested. "It sounds more snappy."

"You could," I said, "*erst* being 'first,' just as it is in modern German. But *whilom* has more the air of *sometime*, I think, while, of course, bespeaking greater erudition."

"Or pretentiousness," Jess added. Hey, how come she gets to be the one who, while knowledgeable, comes across as down-to-earth? I didn't want to play "good logophile–bad logophile" here.

But I ploughed on in usual fashion. "The tastes are different, too, even aside from the register. *Erstwhile* has the *t* stop in the middle, and that *ers* almost sounds like hitting the brakes before it. It also calls forth *first* by rhyme as well as the German connection. *Sometime* starts with a hiss, and calls forth a common word with its own implications – *sometimes* being used variously for 'never' and 'almost always.' *Whilom* is softer and rounder, a glide, a liquid, a nasal; a word to put a baby to sleep. For a while. To while away time. *Why* not?"

"There can be a voiceless glide in it, too," Jess pointed out. "If you really say it as a *wh* word."

"Which we whilom did," I added.

"And you do from time to time," Margot pointed out. "But, say, none of these words can be used just to mean 'from time to time' or 'temporary, at whatever time.'"

"Naw," I said, "I think we're stuck with *temporary* for that. And *momentary*. And various phrases." But I looked over at Jess and she had a heck of a glint in her eye. Her hands dived into her purse; there was a sound like a raccoon trying to escape a junkheap avalanche, followed by the prestidigitation of a small notebook, which Jess opened and

11

thrust forth as though it held a pearl picked up off the sidewalk. Which was not too far from the truth.

"It's obsolete, of course," she said, her voice taking on a slight hush. "But revive it next time you want to say 'temporary' – or should I say 'time-turning.'" We leaned forward to the lambent bond paper and pronounced the pencilled treasure that described its own transit in the English language: "*Whilwendlic*."

moribund

I STOPPED BY MY FRIEND MAURY'S PLACE the other day just as he was anticipating the results of some baking. As I entered, I thought I caught a whiff of scorched cake. I ranged myself against a counter to watch him exhume a fluted tube pan from its crematorium. As Maury inverted the Bundt cake – what was left of it – on a rack, I opened my mouth to comment, and he turned and said, tensely, "Don't-even-say-it."

But *moribund* has a certain something to it, doesn't it? It seems to have *more rebound* than some words (even if its objects have missed their final rebound), with the lips–tongue–lips–tongue, and nasal–liquid–stop–nasal and stop. If you say it in the usual fashion, with the *i* lax and underpronounced, it's quite dominated by some of the more sepulchral vowel sounds we have, especially with the nasal. It's a word headed for death, and stopping at the [d] (because I could not stop for death, it kindly stopped at d…). Of course, it's seldom used literally now; it's more likely seen with such as *economy* and *industry*.

I reflected further as I scanned Maury's interior decorations. He had a picture of the old European riverfront section of Shanghai, famous for its commerce and nightlife in the 1930s, moribund under Mao, now very much on the rebound: a river of bright lights, in fact. "Nice picture of the Bund, Maury," I said. He peered at me over the tops of his glasses.

My vision strayed to the splayed flowers in a dish on his table. "Moribana?" I asked. They did not seem to be doing so well; they were perhaps closer to icky than to ikebana. Maury strolled over, looked at the flowers – bound for glory, as the saying goes, only without the glory – and looked at me. And didn't say anything. At. All.

Well, it must be difficult for Maury, having a name that recalls the Latin root for "die," *mori*. I try to be sensitive; I've stopped calling every gift and postcard I get from him a *memento Maury*. But he doesn't make it any easier for himself, either.

13

On this particular day, he wanted to show me a new tuxedo he'd bought. He came out from his bedroom in the full-on suit complete with cummerbund and black bowtie (real, not clip-on, give the guy credit), and he was holding a martini glass. "Bond," he said, "Maury Bond."

And then paused. And winced.

I pointed at his waistine, of which there was more than before, and, indicating the pleated cloth thereon, asked, "Moribund?"

He raised his martini hand. Straightened his arm. Pointed his index finger to the door.

"One *more pun*, and…"

He sighed, gave up, and went to refill his glass.

biweekly

MAURY, PHILIPPE, AND I, in our student days, had a custom of taking tea with the lovely Liza. I showed up every Saturday, and every Saturday Philippe was also there. Only every second Saturday did Maury show up. One such Saturday, as we were sitting sipping tea while Liza had gone to the kitchen to fetch some cookies, I asked Maury, "Why is it that you only come every other Saturday?"

"What do you mean?" he said. "We all do. Don't we?"

"Well, Philippe and I are here every Saturday."

"Yes," said Philippe, "and why is it that you lads don't show on Wednesdays?"

I turned to Philippe, an exclamation mark hanging over my head. "Wot! You come twice a week?"

"Well, certainly," Philippe said with a little shrug. "It's what she said we were to do. Don't you remember?"

"What I remember," said Maury, clinking his teacup onto the saucer, "is that she said, 'Come biweekly.'"

"Well, yes," I said. "Come by weekly."

"But certainly it was 'come biweekly,'" Philippe affirmed, making that palms-up "obviously" gesture. "And that's what I've been doing."

I looked from one to the other, nonplussed. Just then, the cute and acute Liza reemerged bearing shortbreads. "When you told us to come biweekly," I asked her, "what did you mean?"

The right corner of her mouth canted up; her left eyebrow arched. She swept her eyes over us, alighting them last on Philippe.

"Just what you heard," she replied. "Cookie?"

Since then, I have come to understand how semantics can lead to some antics. But there are few semantics more antic than those of this word. It's not a contronym (like *cleave* and *cleave*), true, but darn close. We know from the Latin-derived *bi* that there are two of something involved, and the Anglo-Saxon *weekly* (from words for "week" and "like") sets the point of reference, but beyond that it's like not knowing the difference between a square and a square root (which, if you're a negative one, can become a real – or imaginary – problem). Clearly this affixation is a match made in heck.

We can avoid it with various circumlocutions, of course. There are even other words, arguably clearer: *fortnightly* (but in Canada we seem not to have fortnights, unless it means sleeping out in your childhood play structure) and *semiweekly* (which, however, to my eyes risks the same misunderstandings).

But the ambiguity does make it useful for play, as do its other properties. It has two doubles in it – a double-u and a double *e* – and the rotating forks at the end (opening rightward on *k* and upward on *y*) may be imagined as relating to a shift of perspective. And of course there are the various puns that can be made on it.

Which takes me back to the tea. Maury and I were feeling like we'd been had, but, more importantly, that we'd been had less often than Philippe. For tea, I mean.

I remembered the axiom that fortune favours the bold. "Well, then," I said, seeing if I could outflank my smooth friend, "what say we do dinner on Fridays? I'll buy weekly."

"I'd gladly treat you Thursdays and Sundays," Philippe riposted. "Biweekly."

Maury, ever the impecunious schlimazel, knew he could not compete. He rose, took his coat, said "Bye" weakly, and left.

molossus, molasses

"No, NO, NO!"

Maury stood fuming, his hands splayed to the air and covered with thick, black, sticky liquid, while more of the same spread at leisure across the counter and dripped viscously onto the floor.

"That's a molossus," I said, getting up to have a better look at the peccadillo.

"I know it's molasses," Maury growled. "It's molasses from a structurally unreliable carton!" He uttered an imprecation that would be indelicate to print here.

I reached over and turned on the kitchen tap, then grabbed a couple of paper towels to help mop up the mess. I was there to eat his food, after all. "No," I said, "what you said. 'No, no, no!' It's a molossus. A foot of three long, or stressed, beats."

Maury was washing his hands. "Who's talking about prosody?"

I risked a pun. "Iamb."

He gave me a persecuted look over the top of his glasses. "Now is not the time for spondee-neity." Heh heh. A true wordplay addict can't resist even when in a sticky situation.

I was stuffing gooey paper towels into his trash can. "What, exactly, are you making, anyway?"

"Shoo-fly pie," he replied. As if on cue, his oven beeped that it was preheated.

"Another molossus!"

"Yes, made with molasses."

"Well," I observed, "in the south, mo' lasses than lads make it."

"Yes," Maury said, tossing the disintegrated carton in the rubbish, "and no doubt you'll next make some point about its colour resembling the nether parts of moles."

"No," I lied, "I was next going to talk about how those southern girls like to call you 'honey,' which, in Latin, is *mel* – a nice nickname for

17

a southern belle – which was the root of *mellacium*, which fed through Portuguese or Spanish to make our molasses." I leaned against the wall as Maury took another carton of molasses out of his cupboard. Who has multiple molasses in their cupboard? And how many did Maury have? He closed the door before I could see.

"I'll have to use blackstrap," he said, and added, apparently forgetting who he was talking to, "so called because when poured it forms a ribbon rather like a black leather strap." As he measured it, he muttered, "I'm heading for more of a black dog here right now."

"A molossus dog," I offered. "Massive, like a mastiff. A now-defunct breed, but a contributor to some of our bigger modern breeds, from St. Bernard to Rottweiler. A toponym: Molossia is a place in northwestern Greece."

"Both words sound heavy," he observed, "but not sticky." He measured some baking soda into the mixing bowl, which held a mix of molasses, water, and eggs, and it frothed gratifyingly, making a slight sound not unlike the [s]'s in the words in question. As he mixed in some crumble of flour, sugar, and butter and poured it all into a pie shell, then topped it with more of the crumble, he mused, "I wonder why a dog. Because it's big? Why not a chimpanzee? That's a molossus."

"Perhaps they simply both come from the same place." I watched him slide the pie into the oven. "Why name musical modes *Lydian*, *Phrygian*, or *Dorian*?"

"Or fridge-doorian." Maury fixed his gaze on the fridge door and I got out of the way. He retrieved the mint syrup and ice for his impending julep and took them to the table, whereon rested the bourbon and glasses. "But nobody much uses those modes now, just as nobody much uses the molossus."

I followed, hot on the trail of my next refreshment. "Gilbert and Sullivan did." I saw Maury's back momentarily freeze. He knew a song cue was coming and there was nothing he could do to stop it. He filled his tumbler to the brim as I launched into *The Mikado*:

"To sit in solemn silence in a dull dark dock,
In a pestilential prison, with a life-long lock,

Awaiting the sensation of a short, sharp shock,
From a cheap and chippy chopper on a big black block!"

Maury turned, washed back half his glass, and appeared to envision me enduring execution. He made an unpleasant smile.

"Yes, yes, yes!"

triptych

"How was Spain?"

I knew this simple question would lead to a treat. Marica and Ronald were a bit of an odd couple and could have two different conversations simultaneously using the same words.

"I loved the triptych," Marica said. For her, the point of any trip was to see art. And she had mentioned she wanted to see Bosch's Haywain triptych in the Museo del Prado, a sure highlight for a medieval fantasist.

"Oh, yeah," Ronald concurred, "the Trip Tik was pretty good. There were some puzzling aspects, but it seemed clear enough by the right edge."

Although Ronald's interest in trip planning always focused on which model of car he would be renting, Marica nonetheless managed to cozen herself into believing he cared about art. "Yes," she said, "such a grand progression: innocence in the beginning, the great hay wagon in the middle, with the Christ" – Ronald snorted – "and then the descent into Hell at the end."

"Well, you're being a bit dramatic about the Madrid traffic, perhaps, but just a bit. But, yeah, I almost forgot that hay wagon. And what I said when I nearly ran into it!"

Marica turned and squinted at him. "Oh, for heaven's sake, you and your driving. I bet you don't even know who's Bosch." She pronounced *Bosch* in the Dutch manner, rather like "boss."

"Obviously," he said, "you are, since I only drive to get you from gallery to gallery! But you're the one who started in about the Trip Tik. I didn't think you even cared about the CAA."

"I don't," she said. "Nasty people who work against public transportation. But what has that to do with – I do say, James, would you like to share something with the class?"

I was nearly convulsing with laughter; I contained myself enough to launch into one of my wonted explanations. "She's talking about a triptych as in a three-panelled painting," I explained to Ronald. "You may perhaps remember a painting on three wooden panels hinged together –"

"More than one of them," Ronald replied. "The place is infested with them. Next thing she's going to want to paint our closet doors. But they don't all have to do with trips."

"Oh," I said, "it's from the Greek *tri*, 'three,' and *ptuché*, 'fold.' Nothing to do with trips. Whereas you're talking about a route guide with tips and tricks for your trip. *Trip* plus *Tik*. No fancy *ych* ending to make it look arcane."

"Or yecchy," Ronald muttered. He added more conversationally, "But my Trip Tik has nothing to do with her triptychs."

"And what, pray tell, would be a *Tik*?" Marica interjected.

"Obviously *triptych* influenced this formation," I said. "They did it more to make it stick than to trip your tongue. But I suspect it was also influenced by the international motoring passport that came out in the early 20th century, the triptyque. Which was a card that folded in three, hence the name. Linear route maps, for their part, have also been around longer than the CAA, AAA, or AA."

"They sure beat a big road atlas," Ronald declared.

"Well," Marica said with contained disdain, "a road atlas is still the only kind of diptych you'll look at."

"Hey!" Ronald looked almost hurt. "I checked the dipstick when we picked up the car! Not my fault the thing developed a leak and we ran out of oil."

inkling

EDGAR FRICK AND MARILYN FRACK appeared to be wrinkling their brows more than usual. And, in fact, their brows appeared to be more than usual. As I neared the leather-clad duo, who were also looking even more than usually feral – yet still urbane – I discerned that they had Star-Trek-derived rubber prostheses on their heads. And their leather suits had somehow managed to acquire a number of loose socks and other light fabric items, apparently (if unbelievably) held on by static.

Well, what the heck. It was the Order of Logogustation's pre-Hallowe'en masquerade. If I could come as ogham (in a rather scratchy suit), they could come as...

"*Kling*-ons," Edgar said, raising his glass of sparkling wine. He tapped it with Marilyn's and they simultaneously chimed "Kling!"

"Oh, yes," Marilyn said, chuckling, "we're having a crackling good time this evening." She made a little frisson that caused her fizzy wine to slosh.

"Careful, dear," said Edgar, "you're sprinkling."

"And apparently you're both pickling," I observed. "But I see you're testing the limits of our truckling and stickling, coming as a pseudo-morpheme."

"Are you heckling?" asked Marilyn, her eyes twinkling.

"Oh, no, no," I said. "Any word taster with so much as a darkling inkling will pick out the tickling of a good pseudo-morpheme. Of course one most usually uses *pseudo-morpheme* to mean something that's a morpheme in one place and appears falsely as one in another, such as *car* in *carpet*."

"But *copter* in *helicopter* can be called one," Edgar pointed out. "And so why not *kling*, which shows up in so many places?"

"Although sometimes across syllable boundaries, and sometimes with a long or even syllabic /l/," I reminded him.

"Well," Marilyn said, "they really all fall into one of two sets: verbs with the frequentative *le* suffix, with *ing* added, like *tinkling*, and nouns ending in *k* that have the diminutive or relational *ling* suffix added, like *duckling*."

"And they have that stop-liquid movement of the tongue that sets your skin prickling," Edgar added, running his finger up Marilyn's spine. Marilyn obliged with another frisson.

"You're certainly not missing the echoes," I said, looking at their static cling and their glasses. "But you *are* missing one word that doesn't fit either pattern."

"Well," Marilyn said, eyebrow arched, "I don't have an inkling what that would be."

"You rather do," I said. "You just said it, in fact."

"But *inkling* comes from *inkle*!" Marilyn protested.

"*Inkle* is really a backformation," I said.

Edgar raised an index finger. "It's you against the *OED*, old boy."

I raised an index finger right back at him. "But even the *OED* gives only two citations that they don't themselves describe as backformations, and they can't say where those come from. Whereas the *American Heritage Dictionary* has a rather anfractuous explanation that follows it from *niche* through *nik*, 'notch' or 'tally,' through *nikking*, meaning 'slight indication' or 'whisper,' to *ningkiling*, which, through false splitting, went from *a ningkiling* to *an ingkiling*, or *an inkling*."

"Well, *that's* a bit of linguistic swashbuckling," Marilyn said, crinkling her nose.

"And we nonetheless have to deal with the *ink*, which is an indisputable pseudo-morpheme," Edgar said. "There's no ink in this word, but who can't think of an ink spot when saying it? Or perhaps a little pen imp peeking from the inkpot?"

"Ah," Marilyn purred, "a darkling little darling."

"And *there's* a word that goes both ways," Edgar said, almost leering. "*Darkling*, such a nice poetic word, suckling at the teat of Erato." (Marilyn gave another frisson and tossed back her sparkling.) "Originally *dark* plus *ling*, but more recently backformed to *darkle*."

"No need to engage in wanton Eraticism while tackling these words, you Greekling," I said.

23

Marilyn winked and stroked the back of a fingernail down my cheek. "Oh, don't be a weakling," she said, cackling.

"We cling? Oh," I replied, "I'm glad to let *you* cling." Which they were. To each other. But they were closing on me, too.

Marilyn gave me an elevator look, and I don't think she was reading my ogham. "Edgarrrrr," she mrowled, "I think someone needs a spankling."

At which point I made myself scarce in a twinkling.

kiwi

THERE WERE FOUR OF US at lunch, and Maury was talking: "I had a kiwi for supper the other day, and—"

Elisa and I interrupted him simultaneously. "You ate an apteryx?" I asked. "That's not very much," Elisa declared. Then Elisa turned to me and said, "An apteryx? *A-pte-ryx*. I like that word. What does it mean? Another word for *kiwi*?"

"Have you ever been a reader of the comic strip B.C.?" Jess asked Elisa. "There's an apteryx in it from time to time, and the first thing it always does is explain what it is: 'a wingless bird with hairy feathers.' It's from Greek *a* 'not' and *pterux* 'wing.' So it is another word for *kiwi*, yes. But probably not the kind you have in mind, and James is being disingenuous."

"Knowing Maury, it seems entirely possible," I said, forestalling another bite of my Cobb salad. "Nor did he say *kiwifruit*, which he probably would for the sake of precision."

Elisa furrowed her brow and looked at her tropical salad. "But *kiwifruit* is just a long way to say *kiwi*, isn't it? Like this." She held up a piece of kiwifruit on her fork.

"Rather," Maury said, "it's a short way to say *Chinese gooseberry*. Like that." He gestured at Elisa's fork.

"This isn't a gooseberry!" Elisa protested.

"No," Jess said, "it's a Macaque peach." She smiled just slightly with the right corner of her mouth. She did have a slight sadistic side underneath all that pleasantness.

"Okay, now I'm lost," Elisa declared, and attacked her salad with renewed vigour.

"Kiwifruits come originally from China," I explained. "When they were introduced to New Zealand, the New Zealanders thought they tasted somewhat like gooseberries, so they called them *Chinese gooseberries*, although they had previously been called a number of other things, including, as Jess says, *Macaque peach*. And several things in different dialects of Chinese."

Elisa swallowed. "So why did they get called *kiwi*? After the New Zealanders?"

"After the bird," Maury said.

"The bird you had for supper?" Jess asked with feigned innocence. She took another bite of her grilled cheese and bacon sandwich.

"She was one of them, yes, in a manner of speaking," Maury said, and picked at the third row of his Cobb salad. (I toss mine together; he keeps his in rows and he objects if it arrives tossed.)

"You guys! Stop it!" Elisa exclaimed. "I feel like I'm the only one not in on the joke!"

Jess took pity. "The apteryx," she explained, "a wingless bird with hairy feathers, is indigenous to New Zealand; in fact, it's the national symbol. The word for it in Maori, the Polynesian language of New Zealand, is *kiwi*, apparently an imitation of its call. New Zealanders are called *kiwis* after the bird. The fruit is called *kiwifruit* perhaps because it looks like the bird – round, brown and hairy – but certainly because it comes from New Zealand. Well, now it does."

"When they started exporting them to America," I added, "China was not seen very favourably. *Kiwifruit* was good marketing."

"But with the ascendancy of the fruit in North America," Maury noted, "the apteryx has become more of an asterisk."

"Where did you guys learn this stuff," Elisa asked, "Kiwipedia?" She smiled at her joke, then licked her lips. "*Kiwi. Ki-wi.* Sounds kinda like *peewee*. Or—" she speared another piece and took it on a roller-coaster ride through the air— "wheee!"

"Or *QE2*," I said, "a cruise ship. Or *QEW*, a highway on which cruise control is largely out of the question. Or maybe *key lime*."

"It looks nice on paper, too," Jess said, "the *k* and *w* all angular at a 90-degree rotation, and the two *i*'s. And it's velum to lips when you say it, almost like a wee kiss."

"Yeah," Elisa said, all happy. She paused. "But wait. You had one for supper? A kiwi bird?" She looked at Maury.

"Yes," he said, "she was from Auckland. Just flew in."

"Well, at least auks fly, unlike kiwis," I said. "But I hope it wasn't awkward."

"No, she was quite pleasant," he declared. "Charming accent. Very happy not to be mistaken for an Aussie."

"*Bird* is New Zealand slang for 'girl,'" Jess explained to Elisa. "Also Australian and British."

The penny dropped. "You had a girl from New Zealand over for supper!" Elisa beamed. "So what did you serve her?"

Maury speared the last piece of his salad and paused it in midair. "Chinese goose."

four very long words

THE ORDER OF LOGOGUSTATION does know how to party... polysyl-labically. One popular event is Night of the Long Words. Its unofficial theme song is "Excellent Birds" (also called "This Is the Picture") by Laurie Anderson and Peter Gabriel, which has the line "Long words. Excellent words. I can hear them now."

We like to bring out some of the old favourites – words and de-bates. Which word to count as the longest word, for instance.

"I am of the opinion that in normal circumstances one may count *antidisestablishmentarianism* as the longest word in the English language as it is spoken today among those words not deliberately coined solely for the sake of being long," opined Raoul Carter at a recent instance of the meeting.

"You've managed to produce a sentence as agglutinative as that word," I noted approvingly.

"Moreso," Raoul said. "There are only seven morphemes in *anti-disestablishmentarianism*, not as many as I had modifying phrases." He was right, too, by one way of counting them anyway: *anti+dis+estab-lish+ment+ari+an+ism*. One cannot decompose *establish*, the stable root of the word, further; it comes, by way of former French *establir* (now *établir*), from Latin *stabilire*, which derives from *stabilis* "stable." Add to it in the following sequence: *disestablishment* (meaning, in this case, separation of church from state), *disestablishmentary* (an adjective form), *antidisestablishmentary* (meaning opposed to this doctrine of disestablish-ment), *antidisestablishmentarian* (of an antidisestablishmentary nature), and finally, as the noun for the belief in this opposition to disestablish-ment, *antidisestablishmentarianism*.

"The problem," my old friend Philippe chipped in, "is that the word really only exists in the language now – only surivived, and per-haps really was motivated in the first place – because of its length. And if you are of the sesquipedalian disposition, then absolutely, without question, undeniably, obviously, *floccinaucinihilipilification* is a longer word on paper."

"Cute," I said. "Another syntax-morphology match-up." Philippe made a small bow of acknowledgement. The first four morphemes of *floccinaucinihilipilification* – *flocci*, *nauci*, *nihili*, and *pili* – all denote insignificant things or nothing and come from phrases (in the *Eton Latin Grammar*) meaning "don't care" – each of the words plus *facere*, "make" (e.g., *flocci facere*). The word as a whole, invented fancifully for the sake of length, refers to the act or habit of estimating something as worthless.

"However, it has one less phoneme," Raoul noted correctly (it has two cases where two letters represent one phoneme – *au* and *ti* – whereas Raoul's word has but one, *sh*).

"And, on the other hand, one more syllable," Philippe parried.

"But if we're to allow words that have been invented to be long," I said, "then you both know that a longer words stalks the lexicon: open your dictionaries to *pneumonoultramicroscopicsilicovolcanoconiosis*." I did not try to mirror the morphology with my syntax.

"Ick," Raoul said. "It's not even very well formed. There's no especially good reason to have it joined between *microscopic* and *silico*. It's like *supercalifragilisticexpialidocious*. It's simply not normal in English to put an *ic* in the middle of a word without so much as a hyphen."

"Besides," Philippe added, dogpiling on, "it's just a surgically enhanced version of *silicosis*. There isn't another single word that expresses either of our words; you need a phrase for each of them."

"If perhaps a shorter phrase," I pointed out.

At this point Jess walked up. "Gents," she said, "there *is* a word of goodly length that was coined entirely in earnest."

"Oh, not that bloody chemical name that requires a paperback book," Raoul said, rolling his eyes.

"No," Jess said, "that's in no dictionary, and if that word exists then one need merely posit a slightly more complex chemical and come up with an even longer 'word' for this hypothetical substance. No, I mean *pseudopseudohypoparathyroidism*. Every bit of it has a reason to be there, even both *pseudos*." True: pseudohypoparathyroidism is a condition that seems like hypoparathyroidism – a parathyroid deficiency – but isn't, and pseudopseudohypoparathyroidism in turn resembles that condition but isn't it.

"Oh, that's just a technical term," Raul said with a wave of his hand.

"Meaning someone actually uses it," Jess countered.

"Funny, though," said Philippe, "nobody ever talks about that one."

"People do tend to shy away from inherited metabolic disorders," I said. "But also, it's not really in the game, as it were. It wasn't coined to be long; it's an accidental competitor."

Raoul, meanwhile, had been silently enunciating while counting on his fingers. "Not if you count phonemes or syllables it doesn't," he said.

"I believe he's floccinaucinihilipilificating your word," Philippe said to Jess.

"It's still a word that is actually used in earnest," Jess said. "And it's smooth and rhythmic."

She had a point. And I leave the further tasting of these words – their mouthfeel and echoes in particular – to the reader as an exercise. Quite a bit of exercise, I'd say.

cachexy

AMID THE AFTERMATH OF verbal bacchanals, a bit of bad bearing can sometimes bring out interesting phonetic effects. One morning after a late night of wine, words, and song, as I was struggling with almond butter on toast, Elisa Lively – who really is, and sometimes a bit too much – came bouncing up with a book.

"Look!" she said, thrusting an open page spread between me and my bread. "*Cachexy!* It's so sexy!"

She pronounced it like "ka-check-see." I felt obliged to correct her. However, with my head thumping and my tongue cleaving to the roof of my mouth, I grimaced out something that was intended to be "ka-keck-see" but involved two phonemes not heard in English, one of them three times: the /k/ realized with not the tip nor the back but the full-on middle of the tongue against the hard palate, and the /s/ made by hissing out the sides of the mouth with the tongue still stuck to the top.

"Oh, yes, 'ka-keck-see,' I see!" she chirped.

"From Greek *kakos*, 'bad,'" I said, having recovered my tongue, "and *hexia*, 'condition.' Means just that: general ill health, malnutrition, that sort of fun. That must be a medical book."

"No, it's philosophy," she beamed. "The author is writing of a *fin-de-siècle Weltschmerz*."

I have a fin-de-semaine Kopfschmerz, I thought, but left it unsaid.

"But," she continued, "say it again! You said it really interestingly!"

"What, *cachexy*? Oh…" I made a weak smile and grimaced out the almond-butter version again. My head hurt a little with every exclamatory *k*.

"Aren't those sounds from Hindi?"

"Well, no, I think the stops in Hindi that are like this are done more with the tip curled back rather than with the body. The hissing *s*, aside from being said in English by some with oral dysfunctions, is like a sound in Welsh, the voiceless lateral, *ll*, only I'm doing it with my teeth clenched, which makes the pitch higher."

"Well, what's really interesting about it —" she made some tries at it, sounding like she was suppressing emesis, which did not serve my guts well: "*k! k! ks!* — is that when you have your tongue full-on pressed like that it tends to make an affricate when you release it."

"Mm-hmm. Yes. So our *x*, which is not an affricate, meets its two parts in the middle and becomes one." I reached for my cup of tea and succeeded in causing it to fall and shatter on the floor. I stood wincing for a moment before searching for something to clean it up with. Elisa observed me and then reached down to help.

"Say," she said, ever the observant one, "you're looking a bit dodgy this morning. I hope it's nothing bad?"

"A bit of a bad condition," I said, trying to wipe up with my eyes half-open. "But transitory. Could be worse. Could be cachexy." I couldn't smile because I was wincing.

She couldn't resist a little play with the sound, which, it turns out, is less charming from the receiving end at the wrong time. "Well, I hope it's not *catching*. Should I call you a *taxi*?"

"No," I said, warming to it in spite of myself. "*Similia similibus curantur*: like cures like. Just pour me a Metaxa."

calque, loanword

"LONG TIME NO SEE!" Marilyn exclaimed untruthfully as I approached. "Here," she said to Edgar, handing him her plate so she could hug me, "take the cake."

"No," he leered, taking it, "you take the cake."

"You both – *unh* – take the cake," I said, as Marilyn crushed me against her leather-clad bosom.

At this point Maury happened by. "I'd say you take the calque," he said.

"Oh," Marilyn exclaimed, releasing me, "is this cake a calque?"

"No," he said, "it's a chiffon cake. Made in a Bundt pan." He made it, so he would know.

"Which makes it two loanwords," I pointed out.

"Indeed. But *takes the cake* is, arguably, a calque – from the Greek. The phrase translates directly from the Greek in Aristophanes."

"Surely," Edgar interjected, swallowing, "the Greeks were not the only people to use cakes as prizes. The term could have come up independently."

"Indeed it could have," Maury said, "like your Adam's apple. But not like *Adam's apple*."

"A calque from the French," I said, with a smiling nod: "*pomme d'Adam*." (Marilyn leaned over to Edgar and murmured something which I suspect was "I'll French your Adam's apple!") "And," I continued, "*long time no see* is a calque from Chinese, exactly word for word. In Mandarin, it's *hao jiu bu jian*. Though *hao* in most contexts would be translated as 'good.'"

"'Good time no see'?" Marilyn cocked her head. "That would sound rather impolite. And unfortunate: not seeing a good time." She gave a calcareous, calculated grin and traced a seam on Edgar's jacket with her red-polished fingernail.

"Tracing is the origin of *calque*," I said, trying to keep their pursuits in the intellectual realm. "French *calque*, noun, 'copy,' comes from *calquer*, verb, 'trace,' which itself traces back to Latin *calcare*, verb, 'tread.'"

"Well, it may look like an elegant word," Marilyn said, "with the *que* and that nice *c* to start, but it sounds like a cat coughing up a furball. Especially if you underpronounce the /l/. I'm glad this cake isn't a calque."

"You're not alone," I said; Maury finished my pun: "But it is." (A loan, of course.) "*Chiffon*, as James pointed out. A French word originally meaning 'rag' but coming to mean a light, diaphanous fabric. And by transference from that, light and fluffy pies and cakes."

"In this case, as made by Maury, Bundt," I added, and got a low-lidded look over the lenses from Maury, who did not wish more *moribund* jokes. But I simply said "From German for 'turban.'"

"*Loanword*," Edgar said, rolling it on his tongue. "There's a nice English formation, ironically. *Loan* plus *word*, both great old Anglo-Saxon four-letter monosyllables. Low and liquid, almost moaning, so unlike *calque*." Marilyn responded predictably to this: she became lower and more liquid and almost moaned as she creaked her leather garments against his while taking their pieces of dessert and setting them on a side table behind him. Maury's eyes rolled... rolled away and he followed them.

"Even more ironic," I said, trying valiantly to maintain a conversation. "*Loanword* is actually taken from German *Lehnwort*."

Marilyn looked up abruptly. "So it's a calque!"

"Yes," I said, "and *calque* is a loanword."

"A semantic exchange," Edgar said, cocking his eyebrow. "An exchange of tongues, as it were." (Marilyn murmured, audibly, "As it will be...") He smiled. "That takes the cake."

Marilyn reached for the side table and came up empty. "Speaking of the cake," she said, "where is it?"

"Maury took it," I said, not without schadenfreude, and headed off to get my own piece.

in excelsis

A CAROL SING IS not always a good idea among word fanatics. Although they provide many wonderful archaic usages to savour, things can get a bit contentious at times. And so I'm frankly not sure what I was doing in late November singing quartets with Daryl, Margot, and Jess.

Actually, I do know. We were rehearsing. Of course you have to rehearse before Advent in order to be ready to sing when people want you to sing. And we were doing "Angels We Have Heard on High" – or was it "Ding Dong Merrily on High"? – when we came up against that perennial choir catch: *excelsis*.

There were four of us. On the first pass, there were four different pronunciations.

"People," Margot said, lowering her music, "don't you know Latin? Never mind how it's been bastardized over the past couple of millennia. *C* is pronounced [k]. 'Eks-kel-cease.'"

"We're not singing classical Latin," I said. "We're singing ecclesiastical Latin. Grammar, vocabulary, and pronunciation changed some in the centuries between the one and the other. Note how we're not pronouncing the English words in fifteenth-century style."

"That's right," Daryl said. "The *c* before *i* and *e* became an alveopalatal fricative. So it's 'ex-chell-cease.'"

Jess and I both winced. (So did Margot, but she does it so often you hardly need to say so.) "That's not quite right, either," Jess said. "While *c* became 'ch' before the front vowels, *sc* became 'sh.' No need for a transition through 's-ch' either. You can also see this transformation in, for instance, Norwegian and Swedish: *ski* is actually said with a fricative, similar to our 'she.' And in ecclesiastical Latin, *xc* before *i* or *e* is 'ksh.' So it's 'ek-shell-cease.' Just sing it all like Italian."

"Or you can go with the English tradition," I added. "I admit I'm not the world's hugest fan at all times of what happened to Latin when it got run through the Great Vowel Shift and all that along with

English – 'nil nice eye bone 'em' for *nil nisi bonum* and all that – but when you look at these songs, they're really English songs with the Latin borrowed in. So you can sing 'ek-sell-cease' just as the guys who wrote the words most likely had in mind."

"Sounds like 'In Excel spreadsheets'!" Margot snorted. "Or 'in egg-shell sheets.' Daryl's version sounds like a cash register or a pachinko machine."

Jess smirked slightly. "And you find your anachronistic stop-laden classical version somehow more euphonious?"

"*Excel* is related, etymologically," I pointed out. "Latin *ex-cellere*, 'rise above others,' with the *cel* related to *celsus*, 'lofty.'" Margot was undoubtedly gratified that I said the Latin the classical way. "*Excelsus* is 'high,' so the English just repeats the Latin anyway: 'on high,' 'in the highest.' Actually, the word used could as easily have been *altissimis* – Saint Jerome preferred that version."

"And then we wouldn't be having this argument," Daryl said.

"We shouldn't anyway," Jess said. "How can anyone hear *in excelsis* without thinking of Christmas? And how can anyone be –"

Margot jumped in: "– anything but stressed out by the pre-Christmas season? Yeah."

"Well," I said, "I'm going to throw my vote in with Jess, so that gives us a plurality, which is enough to win. It's the shell, icky or otherwise. Let's try it again."

We ran through the song again, with Margot giving the grimace we all expected from her at the appropriate point, but going with the decision. As we were singing, Elisa wandered by and stopped to listen.

"How'd we sound?" Jess asked her when we were done.

"Excellent!" Elisa declared. "On key, gives me chills… don't cease!"

mafficking

IT WAS A RIGHT JOLLY NIGHT at Domus Logogustationis, the clubhouse of the Order of Logogustation. Our local branch had prevailed against a hostile acquisition bid on the building that would have driven us into the street. Instead, it was our celebrations that drove us into the street, mucking up the traffic: we no longer needed to camp out watching for padlocks on the doors; the siege had been lifted. Needless to say, we were not behaving like boy scouts – rather more boorishly. Long words (excellent words!) were falling like snow as we careered tantivy into the laneway. Elisa Lively twirled along the sidewalk singing "Supercalifragilisticexpialidocious" until overtaken by hypoxemia.

"What are you doing?" a passer-by asked.

"Mafficking," Philippe Entrecote replied.

"What?"

Ross Ewage, the noted vulgarian, leaned over. "As in 'Keep yorficking hands off mafficking building!'"

"As Baden-Powell might have said, yes," Philippe said, nodding smoothly.

The passer-by moved on in that quick-stepping way people do when they conclude they have been talking to a dangerously crazy person. Ross turned to Philippe. "Baden-Powell? As in the founder of the Boy Scouts?"

"Yes, it was he who held Mafeking during the siege. Two hundred seventeen days, hemmed in by the Boers. He used cute subterfuges such as having his men place fake land mines while the Boers were watching them – and stepping and ducking to avoid imaginary barbed wire. The Boer War was basically a white-against-white war, but Baden-Powell put three hundred native Africans on the perimeter with guns."

"To get shot first, no doubt," Ross said, as a cava cork traced gravity's rainbow past his ear. ("Sorry!" shouted Maury.)

"Rather. He also put together a cadet corps of adolescent boys. That helped inspire the Scouts, which he formed seven years later when he was back in England."

"So mafficking really wasn't just partying but mayhem – a battle! The Siege of Mafeking!"

"Actually, the verb *maffick* was backformed on the basis of the celebrations when the siege was lifted, May 17, 1900. Naturally the British citizens in Mafeking were very happy to see the departing backsides of their Boerish opponents. The celebration spread rather far, certainly across South Africa to Cape Town, and, I believe, even to London. It was a major victory in the war. Waggish journalists reporting the celebrations spoke of 'maffickers, mafficking as hard as they could maffick.'"

"And the neighbours," Ross said, "were probably saying 'Those rotten ma-fickers.'" He might have pronounced it slightly differently, come to think of it.

Elisa spun to a stop and grasped Philippe's shoulder for stability. "Language!" she shouted, but it wasn't clear if she was chastising Ross or simply exulting.

"We're talking of *mafficking*," Ross said.

"Change the affix and make it *maffICKS*!" Elisa shouted. "Let us maffick in the traffic!" she sang to the tune of "Roll Me Over in the Clover."

"Read the *f*'s as long *s*'s," Maury said, leaning over, "and you have *Massic*, an ancient Italian wine."

"If you could degeminate and change it to *g*, it would be *magick*," Ross said.

"It would," Philippe said, "not least because *f* to *g* is not a known transformation."

"It's a typo!" Elisa shouted into his ear. She grabbed the cava from Maury. "You need some more of this!"

"Make like Tantivy Mucker-Maffick," Maury said. "To quote Thomas Pynchon: 'Tantivy's been drunk in many a place, From here to the Uttermost Isle, And if he should refuse any chance at the booze, May I die with an hoary-eyed smile!'"

"But," Ross half-shouted, "what the f*** does *Mafeking* mean? I mean the place name! Where they had the siege!"

"It's actually Setswana," Philippe said. "It's originally, and now again, *Mafikeng*, and it means 'place of stones.'"

At this Elisa and Maury burst into song, the Rovers hit from the early '80s: "Oh, why don't we all just get stoned… Get drunk and sing beer-drinking songs…" They continued up the street in raucous jubilation. We all mafficked so hard we might have been mistaken for sports fans, except we were in Toronto and nonetheless had something to celebrate.

nautilus

"HELLO, SAILOR! WHAT'S THAT?"

Marilyn Frack creaked as she leaned forward in her black leather outfit to peer at my wrist, or rather at what was on it.

"It's a nautilus," I said. In fact, it wasn't: it was a watch with a ceramic nautilus-shell pattern as its face. But pragmatics allows for brevity.

"It's naughty lust?" she said. "Fie! We'll have none of that!" Her coquettish smile and tone made it clear she really meant "nothing other than that."

"Indeed," I said, trying to be as dry as I could, "we *will* have none of 'fie.' Although the spiral of the nautilus shell is often thought to be a golden spiral, expressing the 'golden mean' ratio, *phi*, it is in fact a logarithmic spiral."

She straightened up a little. "Which means?"

"Which means that each chamber is geometrically similar to each other chamber – the same proportions but different size. An infinite logarithmic spiral will look identical at any magnification."

Edgar Frick wandered up; I hoped his presence would detach his paramour from me slightly. Marilyn may not have a grip quite like that of the nautilus's tentacles, which cling so tightly to prey that they will sooner rip from the nautilus's body than from the prey, but she is indefatigably flirtatious.

"Do I hear something about a Mandelbrot set?" Edgar said.

"Another fractal geometry," I replied.

Marilyn creaked up against Edgar's matching leather kit. "He's trying to nottle us."

"Would I be so shellfish?" I protested.

"Look, darling," Marilyn said, showing Edgar my watch, "it's an endless succession of similar chambers."

"Like our last vacation," Edgar said.

"That did spiral out of control." Marilyn paused. Then smiled.

"The nautilus," I said, returning to my watch if possible. "A free-swimming cephalopod. It can adjust its buoyancy and propel itself by intaking and expelling water."

"How did they come to name a weight machine after it?" Edgar mused.

"The machine controls resistance with the aid of a spiral cam," I replied.

"So it's not because you really have to shell out for one," Marilyn said. She turned to Edgar. "Luscious, how much did ours cost, with the after-market leather add-ons?"

"About as much as a nuclear submarine," Edgar replied. He knew that I knew that he knew that the first nuclear submarine was the USS Nautilus, just one in a series of many vessels named the Nautilus, including not only the submarine in Jules Verne's 1870 novel *Twenty Thousand Leagues Under the Sea* but its namesake, the first actual practical submarine, launched in 1800.

I could see the wheels spinning inside Marilyn's head. I almost broke into a cold sweat as I considered she might be about to launch into a line of discourse relating to rigid cylinders and seamen.

But instead of a cute observation, she made a rather acute one. "*Nautilus* comes from the Greek for 'sailor,' yes?" Edgar and I both nodded agreement. "So these various submarines called *Nautilus* are sailors containing sailors, recursive, the smaller inside the bigger, but similar and repeating. Vaguely reminiscent of a nautilus shell."

"Yes," I said, relieved and impressed. "That's a rather entertaining line of thought. And submarines probably have Nautilus machines on them for exercise. And of course they have other features like nautiluses: buoyancy and propulsion, and perhaps the inner structure…"

"A long succession of chambers with seamen in them," Marilyn said, leering at Edgar and sweeping her hands over him.

"…Look at the time," I declared, glancing perfunctorily at the hands sweeping over the nautilus on my wrist. And escaped.

ouche

"Ouch!"

Jess held up a brooch encrusted with stones of indeterminate preciousness.

I looked at it. "Did you stab yourself?"

"No," she said, "I just wanted to broach the subject. Do you like my ouche?"

"May I touch it?" I replied.

"That sounds louche," she observed.

"Touché."

She handed me the ouche. Yes, *ouche*, also spelled *ouch*, is a term – used now mostly poetically and as a deliberate archaism, but found in such luminous sources as Shakespeare, Kipling, Bulwer-Lytton, and the King James Bible – for a clasp, brooch, or buckle set with precious stones. (*Brooch*, for its part, is in origin the same word as *broach*; two divergent senses – the piercing and the ornamented piercer – took on divergent spellings.)

"It's shaped like an *O*, you see?"

"Like an *O-you-see-H*?" I volleyed back.

"Do you want a jewel?" she said. Or maybe it was "Do you want to duel?" They sound so similar, especially if the person has any British tinges in their pronunciation.

Either way, the best I could give back was "I think you'd have me pinned." I looked at it. "Will you wear it on an apron?"

She smiled. "An orange one." She, of course, knew that *an ouche, an apron*, and *an orange* came originally from *a nouche, a napron*, and *a norange*. It's just another way our language has of making *n*'s meet, eh? She added, "But I might wear it out. Sh!" She raised a finger to her lips.

"Where did you get it?" I asked. "It looks like a bit of an 'ouch' in the wallet."

"Oh," she said, waving it away with a flip of her hand, "I had a voucher."

"Well," I said, handing it back, "don't lose it in the couch."

"Sofa, so good," she said, pinning it on. Then "Ow! Affricate."

"Yes," I said, "it's 'ow' followed by a voiceless affricate. Makes a bit of a moue."

Her mouth was indeed in a moue – sucking her fingertip. "No," she replied, "I said, 'Ah, frick it.' I poked myself."

"Ouch," I said in sympathy. Or perhaps just to needle her.

obnubilate

"I HAVE ONLY THE VEGAS MEMORY," Maury said. Or perhaps it was "vaguest." His eyes were hazing in that way that indicates the beginning of a recounting. "It was late," he continued, "and she was nubile."

I felt myself privileged finally to hear Maury tell the tale, so often adumbrated but so rarely revealed, of his brief marriage.

"It was a Lebanese restaurant. No – Algerian; they were playing nuba music. I was nibbling a bit. Through the haze – *ob Rauch, ob Nebel* – I glimpsed a figure, obnubilated." (Maury does not limit himself to English in his periphrastic peregrinations; the German he said meant "whether smoke or cloud.") "I did a belated double-take; she had eluded my gaze. But when I turned back to my libation, I was elated to see her coming my way. I say elated because she was, in this lugubrious tableau, a jubilee, a liberation. I invited her to sit, and introduced myself. She said her name was Luba. I observed that it reminded me of *ya vas lyublyu*" – Russian for "I love you," as Maury knew I knew. "She was bubbly but knowledgeable. We ate, and libated, and debated; it was ennobling. By evening's end it was indubitable: we did not dabble; we were a couple. We went to the chapel."

Maury stared off into the near distance. I waited. "Well?" I asked at length.

"It is no coincidence that *obnubilate* and *nubile* – and *nuptials* – sound similar," he said. "Latin *nubere*, 'wed,' shares a root with *nubilum*, 'cloud,' apparently through the idea of veiling. Indeed, my eyes were veiled metaphorically just as she was veiled – obscured, obnubilated – literally. We had chosen, as our music, Pink Floyd's *Obscured by Clouds*; it proved to be apposite, not only because of the obnubilation of thought and vision but because I found myself soon thereafter on the dark side of the moon."

"How so?"

"She was nobility, and her family, on hearing the news, mobilized. 'Noblesse oblige!' It seems a lowly plebe was not suitable. Our ring was no longer a dollar-store bauble; it was the veritable baleful band of the Nibelungen. They saw their world in rubble if I did not enable annullment. Luba and I, in the light of day, saw our position as impossible with their opposition. We abjured, annihilated."

Another pause followed. After a suitable wait, I asked, "Do you remain in touch?"

"In touch? No, alas. (Did I mention her nubility?) No further touching could be possible. But we have remained in word. We exchange letters every so often." He held up his French cuffs to display links, Scrabble tiles: L and M. "She sent me these for my birthday."

missile

Pow! A SNOWBALL CONNECTED with my skull behind my right ear. I turned to see young Marcus Brattle, one of England's less staid exports, already making another.

"Like a missile!" He said.

"Enough with misconstrued *similes*," I said. "Not *like* one. It *was* one. Something that's thrown can be called a missile, though we use the word mostly for rockets these days."

"No, but like a *ballistic* missile!"

"It *was* ballistic. You threw it; its course was not under continuous correction. *Ballistic* comes ultimately from Greek *ballein*, to throw" – at this point I ducked his next snowball and he started to scoop snow for another – "and *missile* comes from the past tense of Latin *mittere*, to send or throw. So *ballistic missile* is a tautology – and an etymologically paradoxical name for something that is not thrown but launched under its own power, and that in more recent times may have continuous guidance systems."

"Yes, well," said Marcus, hurling his next projectile and forcing another evasive manoeuvre on my part, "every time I *miss I'll* make another one. Whereas you, apparently, are stuck hurling prayer books."

He was referring to my North American pronunciation of *missile* with a schwa in the second syllable, making it sound like *missal*. "You know," I said, "in the nineteenth century British dictionaries also gave my pronunciation as the only one. The 'long i' version didn't crop up until about a century ago."

"Right," he said, hurling another, giving me cause, as it cruised past my hat, to consider whether my pacifist approach was really effective here, "we finally got it right. 'Cause we don't think hurling and churches necessarily go together."

I looked for, and did not see, an effective missile shield. I continued to try the disarming power of facts. "*Missal* comes from the same Latin root as *missile*, though," I pointed out, "albeit by a less direct route: the word *missa*, 'mass' as in Catholic, comes from the same verb, perhaps from the sending away of catechumens before the eucharist –" Marcus hurled another with a shout of "Away, catechumen!" – "perhaps –" I leapt aside as it scudded by – "from the dismissal of the congregation at the end: *Ite, missa est.* That past participle became a noun and from that the adjective *missal* was formed, which has given many a Canadian Catholic the occasional bellicose pun."

"Well, I'm aiming for your *dis*-missal," Marcus said, hurling on the *dis*.

"You could be on a sticky wicket, sport," I said, gradually drawing nearer to him.

"I'll make this missile whistle – past your ear!" He hurled another and indeed narrowly missed my left ear. "And now –" he started packing one more carefully. I considered my options for missile defense. He held up his ball, which was a rough cube. "The cubin' missile crisis!" he shouted. I leapt forward, took it in the chest at close range, and promptly put him in a headlock.

"Hey!" he said, as I squeezed my biceps against his cranium. "What's that got to do with this? You're changing the topic!"

"It's a guided muscle," I replied, and gave him a good grind on the scalp with my knuckles.

pattern

I WAS ON MY WAY HOME from the World Congress of Logogustation. I looked out the airplane window. Little lines of frost were making a lacy pattern on the glass. I was in a position to peruse them at leisure, as we were in a holding pattern caused by a weather pattern. Funny, I was delayed by weather last year around this time, too… it's getting to be a pattern.

The frost, anyway, was all I had left to look at. The movies and other entertainment were done and the monitor in front of me offered little more than a choice of test patterns. I'd read through the magazine the airline provided for its patrons: the science section on pattern recognition, the psychology section on behaviour patterns, the sports section with its analysis of defensive patterns in football, the puzzles in the back in their various grid patterns… There wasn't a whole lot to look at beyond the seat upholstery pattern. Which, on inspection, held a spatter pattern from someone's coffee… turbulence, perhaps? Over the top of the seat I could see a reflection on the head of an evident victim of male pattern baldness.

I glanced over at the passenger on the aisle side of me, a woman around 30 years old. Her lap was covered with a quilt that she had, with foresight, brought, and she was working on some needlepoint, resting it on a box that apparently held her needles and thread. Under the box I noticed a book of dress patterns.

"That's an interesting pattern," I said.

"Which one?" she asked. She held up the needlepoint and a corner of the quilt.

"That one," I said, pointing with my left hand at the box, which was done in a sort of diamond pattern, with floral patterns winding in and around, rather like a Harlequin being eaten by ivy. She lifted the needlework and I saw a unicorn in the middle of the box lid.

She half-smiled and indicated the unicorn. "That's my patronus. You know, Harry Potter. If some needlework is going seriously awry, I say, 'Expecto patronum!'"

"Does it work?"

"It seems to," she said. "Anyway, it's quicker than a Pater Noster." She looked at my left hand, specifically the ring finger. "Now, *that's* a nice pattern." She pointed at my gold and silver wedding band, which has poinsettias cut into it all around.

"My wife has one just like it," I said.

"I really like that you're not afraid to wear a ring like that. To think that guys used to not wear rings at all... so paternalistic. I'm so glad we've escaped those old patriarchal patterns."

"It's not surprising that patterns would be patriarchal," I mused, "or that the patriarchy would have a pattern. *Pattern* does come from *patron*, which comes from Latin *patronus*, which in turn derives from Latin *pater*, 'father.' *Pattern* first meant a guide or example." I indicated her book of patterns.

She looked at her unicorn, a vague queasiness downturning her mouth. "I kind of wish you hadn't told me that. My unicorn is supposed to be a father figure now?" She looked at her various appurtenances. "And my sewing patriarchal, and my..." I sensed an *aaagh* might be coming.

"Naw," I said quickly. "Meanings change. Established forms and patterns persist but are turned to new uses. Many of the words you now use meant something at least a little different, if not completely different, centuries ago. Think of it as co-optation. Or subversion. After all, you're a patron of this airline."

A little smile returned to the corner of her mouth. "And I wouldn't want to be a matron of it."

"Just to give you an example," I continued, "do you like Gilbert and Sullivan?"

"Oh, yes," she said, "*The Mikado* and *Iolanthe* and *The Pirates of Penzance* – some of my favourites."

"You like their patter songs, then? 'Modern Major General' and all that?"

"Yes. ...Wait. Are those supposed to be *pattern* songs?"

49

"No, but the word *patter* meaning 'rapid speech' comes from the rapid way people used to say certain prayers..."

Now she was really smiling. "Such as the *Pater Noster*!" She set her work on her box and patted it happily. "I think I see a pattern developing."

magi

Epiphany Sunday found us drinking coffee: me, Daryl, Margot, and Jess. "I remember," I said, "when I was growing up in Alberta, one reason we gave that the nativity couldn't have happened there was that we could never get three wise men from the east."

"I wonder," Daryl offered, "whether that had any influence on Richard Gwyn when he title his book on Pierre Trudeau *The Northern Magus*."

"The northern maggots?" Margot snorted. "*May*-gus, not *mag*-us!"

"Trust Margot to cry Fowles," Jess said. I'm not certain that everyone at the table knew that *The Magus* was a book by John Fowles, but no further was made of it. Jess relaxed back to maximize her quality time with the mound of whipped cream on her beverage.

"That's an interesting word, isn't it, *magus*?" I said. "Much more commonly seen in the plural: *magi*. Or *magi*." The first time, I said "may-jye"; the second, "madge-eye." Naturally, Margot snorted at that. "Now, Mair-jo," I said, deliberately riffing on her name, "I'm surprised that you don't prefer 'ma-goose' and 'magee,' which are, after all, the Latin pronunciations."

"I'll toss this one back to you," she said. "You're the one who likes to point out that these words are now English words. So it's been in the language long enough for the vowels to have shifted."

"And now we are seeing another shift," I replied. "Pronunciation of many Latin-derived or otherwise foreign-derived words is going towards a less anglicized style, like it or not. *Data* is often said 'dat-a' rather than 'day-ta,' for instance, and you'll hear 'rash-owe' rather than 'ray-show' sometimes for *ratio*." ("Yuck," Margot interjected.) "And then there's *Kahlil Gibran* and *Genghis Khan*, both of which were originally pronounced with 'j' where the *G*'s are and were spelled that way due to old-style transliteration, but now we see them and think that since they're not English the *G*'s should be 'g'."

"Just like 'fun guy' for the plural of *fungus*," Daryl said. "I mean, if we're going to say the *i* as 'eye,' why wouldn't we say the *g* as 'j'?"

"Exactly!" Margot said. "Every reason to say 'may-jye.'"

"Every reason except that the pronunciation seems to be shifting," I said. "Oh, I'm not saying your pronunciation is wrong; it's the dictionary version. There's no question that it's the formally correct way."

"Thank you!" Margot said, rapping her cup on the table so hard it made a little geyser through the hole in the plastic lid. Jess interrupted her whipped-cream reverie to hand Margot a serviette or two.

"Could the shift be under the influence of *magic*?" Daryl mused.

Margot looked at him as if he had lost his mind. "What? Some wizards waving their wands make the vowels change?"

"*Magic* is cognate with *magus*," Jess pointed out. "In fact, it's almost surprising that we don't pronounce it 'may-jic.' Like an adjectival form of *mage*, though actually it comes by way of Greek *magiké tekhné*."

"Maggie Kay!" Daryl said, echoing the Greek. "Sounds like a nickname for our Margot!"

"Oh, stop," said Margot. "*Maggie* makes me think of *Maggi*, the German answer to soy sauce. Then again, so does the coffee here sometimes." She looked at Jess's cup. "Not that one, though."

Daryl looked at Jess's beverage, which appeared to have chocolate and nut sprinkles on the nearly-gone whipped cream. "What *is* that, anyway?"

"It's an *Oh Henry!* latte," she said. "A veritable gift of the magi." Again, I cannot feel certain that all present recalled that "The Gift of the Magi" is a short story by O. Henry.

"That would explain your adoration of it," Margot remarked dryly. She turned to me. "I don't cotton to your idea that somehow a pronunciation can be formally incorrect but still acceptable. It's right or it's wrong!"

Jess smiled. "We may have a veritable magus among us," she said. "After all, a magus, originally, was a member of the Zoroastrian priestly class. The word comes barely altered from Old Persian – of course the plural is Latinized. But as you may know, Zoroastrianism is a dualistic religion: the world is in conflict between the pure good, the one

God, the ultimate creator, *Ahura Mazda,* and the forces of evil, led by *Ahriman.*"

"Which means," I commented, "that when Margot makes one of her all-or-nothing pronouncements, we may say, 'Thus spoke Zarathustra.'"

"And hope," Jess replied, "she doesn't remember that the reference there is not to the real prophet Zoroaster, also called Zarathustra, but to Nietzsche's version of him, who goes around proclaiming that God is dead."

"Nietzsche is dead," I responded. "But you're right, we don't want to wander into the ideas of the Übermensch and all that proto-Nazi junk."

"Say," Daryl said, "apropos of nothing, it occurs to me that Alberta finally got its own. Just going back to what you said about wise men coming from the east, they sent Stephen Harper to the east as their western magus."

"Except," I said, "Stephen Harper grew up in Toronto. So however you look at it, it's ironic."

"Well," said Margot, "isn't that an epiphany!"

pale

"I TRIPPED THE LIGHT FANDANGO, turned some cartwheels across the floor…" Elisa paused and shrugged. "But apparently I was supposed to stick with the pole, because the instructor said, 'Pal, that's beyond the pale.'"

Maury raised an eyebrow. "In a pole dancing class? That's hardly harem protocol." He took a sip of his pint of pale and grabbed some peanuts from the pail on the table. We were at a Mexican-bar-style pub that also served Spanish food.

"Far from it, I'm sure," I said. "In such a performance, the pole *is* the pale."

"Well," Elisa said, "I didn't have much at stake." She shrugged again and smiled insouciantly.

"But you *were* at a stake," I said. "The pole is a stake, because a stake – a boundary stake, especially – is a pale. Latin *palus*, originally a stake that stood in for an opponent in practice sparring, but then a boundary stake, and then the area enclosed by a boundary." I reached to the tray the waitress had brought and took another drink.

"As in the Pale of Settlement," Maury added, "which was in Russia the area in which Jews were allowed to live. Or the English Pale, which was the British-occupied turf in Ireland, beyond which dwelt all those terrifying Celts."

"*Beyond the pale*, the metaphor, seems to have come from a general reference to the use of *pale* to designate a a safe area, rather than as a specific reference to either of those," I said, and picked a peanut from the pail. "That's how the evidence goes, anyway." Crunch.

"So is *pole* cognate with *pale*, then?" Elisa asked.

"Yep," Maury and I replied simultaneously.

"An how about *pail*," she asked, shaking the bucket.

"Nope," Maury said, and had another pull of his pale.

"But your kneecap is," I said, "and so will my supper be, when it arrives. *Patella* and *paella*."

"My supper would be related to your pole, if they had shish kebabs," Maury mused. "Impaled. But my ale is not. That kind of *pale* comes from Latin *pallidum*."

"The more popular kind of pale, for sure," I said. "*Pale blue, pale yellow, pale green, pale pink; pale face, pale skin, pale eyes*... All the most common collocations. The post kind pales in comparison."

"*Pale Fire*," added Maury, ever the Nabokov fan.

The waitress brought a plate of nachos mounded with melted cheese. "There's another kind of *pale*," Maury said: "A cheese scoop. From a French word for 'shovel'."

"Say," said the waitress, looking at Elisa, "weren't you in the pole-dancing class?"

Elisa looked up and blenched slightly. "Yes!" She looked at the waitress for a moment and recognized her. "You were two poles down, weren't you?"

"That's right! You, me, and the sixteen vestal virgins." She smirked and turned to me and Maury. "Your friend here is a wild one."

"Yes," Maury said, "she seems to have managed a bit of a blot on her escutcheon, we understand."

"If you're talking heraldry," I said, "better to say she has a pale on it now." I looked at Elisa and the waitress. "A vertical bar." The waitress looked at me uncertainly. I was afraid she was about to cut me off. "Anyway," I added, "we know she's quite lively."

That was Elisa's cue. "That's my name!" she burbled. "Elisa Lively." She extended her hand to the waitress.

"Shelly Miller," the waitress said, shaking hands. "Hey, your food's about ready, but you guys —" she turned to me and Maury — "did she tell you about where her shirt ended up?"

We looked up, eyebrows arching. "I think she was about to get to that," I said, suppressing a wicked smile.

"I'll come back when it's calmed down a little and fill in any missing details," Shelly said. She leaned a little towards Elisa and said, in a loud whisper, "I think something of yours ended up in my bag." Elisa smiled, but she was beginning to look kinda seasick.

And so it was, much later, as Shelly Miller told her tale, that Elisa's face, at first just ghostly, turned a whiter shade of pale...

mucous, mucus, nauseous

MUCOUS MAKES ME NAUSEOUS.

At the sight of this sentence, the hairs on Margot's neck stood straight up. She pushed the paper back towards her student, Marcus, and, jabbing her finger at the sentence, said "That's wrong."

"No it's not," he said. "It really makes me sick. Can't stand to look at other people's snot."

"No," said Margot, feeling vaguely queasy, due more to the grammatical infraction than to the imagery, "you have two incorrect usages in that sentence. Here —" she pointed to *Mucous* – "you've used an adjectival form where you should use a noun. The noun *mucus* is spelled *m-u-c-u-s*."

Marcus scratched out the sentence and rewrote it: *Mucus makes me nauseus.*

"No," Margot said, "now you have *mucus* right but there's no such word as *nauseus* without the *o*. It has to be an adjective."

"But you said it was wrong!" Marcus protested.

Sigh. "It's the wrong word there. *Nauseous* should not be used to mean 'nauseated'; it means causing, not feeling, nausea. You could write *mucus is nauseous.*"

Marcus pulled a face. "That's really gross! That sounds like the mucus is about to puke!"

"But using *nauseous* to mean 'feeling sick' is a mark of an insufficiently educated user," Margot said primly.

"Try telling that to my mother," Marcus replied.

"Your mother is paying me to improve your English. If she were paying me to improve hers as well, I would. Now, you could say *mucus nauseates me*. That avoids the issue altogether."

"You know," Marcus said, looking at the paper, "I don't like that, *mucus* without the *o*. I think it looks slipperier and grosser with the o. Also without it it looks too much like my name."

"Well," explained Margot with obvious patience, "it's a noun-adjective distinction. The *o* before the *u* makes it an adjective. Like *callous* and *phosphorous*."

"So I could become an adjective if I added an *o* in my name," Marcus said. "*Marcous*. …What's an adjective?"

Margot paused for a moment to decide exactly when to have the splitting headache she could see in her future. "An adjective," she said, eyes closed, hand on forehead, "is something that modifies a noun. So you have a *callus* on your hand, no *o*, but you exhibit *callous indifference* with an *o*."

"And *calloused hands*, with an *o*, right?"

"No, because in that case you're taking a noun and making it an adjective with the *ed*. So *callus* with no *o* gets the *ed* to be *callused*. Likewise, *phosphorous* with an *o* means 'containing phosphorus' or 'glowing.'"

"So," Marcus said, nudging the paper forward, "this is *Marcous writing*, with an *o*."

Margot almost smiled. "Unfortunately, we can't do that with proper nouns. Names, like yours."

Marcus pursed his lips. "Nothing wrong with a bit of fun now and then," he muttered. Pause. "So where do we see *mucous* with an *o*? Like 'I don't want that Kleenex, it's all mucous?'"

Margot was about to say something and then realized that what she was about to say was not true. "Em… you could. They might not understand you. The most common place to see *mucous* with an *o* is *mucous membrane*, a membrane in your body that has mucus as an essential part of it. Like the inside of your nose."

Marcus remembered something. "Or *mucous relief*."

"No, in that case it's *mucus* with no *o* because it's really what's being relieved – like *cough suppressant*: *cough* is a noun, not an adjective. If it were *mucous* with an *o*, it would suggest that the relief itself was like mucus, or had mucus in it."

"I don't think you're right about that," Marcus said.

Margot opened her mouth in astonishment at the impudence and was about to set him right on the likelihood of his knowing better than her. He held up a finger. "Hang on." He jumped up, went into the bathroom, and reappeared in record time. He was holding a bottle of cough syrup, which proclaimed itself *Mucous and Phlegm Relief.*

Margot took the bottle in her hand, stared at it, and, trying not to hurl it through the nearest window, trying not to scream, and with an overwhelming sense of betrayal, hyperventilated herself to unconsciouness.

Poor Margot. Hard to blame her when a rule of usage proclaimed by all the dictionaries and taught as revealed truth is wantonly trashed by a very large corporation. But the poor lass didn't even get to expostulate on the origins of *mucus* and *nauseous*; by the time the smelling salts were brought out and she came to with that splitting headache she had seen coming down the street, the hour was over.

Well, *mucus* isn't a difficult one; it's Latin, straight down – spelled the same, with the same meaning. *Mucous* is from Latin *mucosus*, which could also mean 'slimy'. You may remember a slimy glue called *mucilage* that you used in rubber-tipped bottles in kindergarten and elementary-school days. That's also derived ultimately from *mucus*. (*Marcus*, for its part, is not related.) You may find something gluey about the [mju] or [miw] at the beginning of *mucus*, and the [k] may bring to mind the closed and phlegmy velum one gets when one has a cold. You may or may not agree with Marcus that it's slimier with an *o*.

Nauseous, for its part, comes (as you may now guess) from *nauseosus*. Of course, there is no *nauseus* and never was; the noun is *nausea*. (Needless to say, *Mucus makes me nausea* is not good.) As to whether one ought to use *nauseous* to mean 'nauseated', well, be aware that many people will consider you not merely wrong but grossly ignorant and offensive if you do. People can be so touchy about language. And indeed, Latin *nauseosus* means 'causing nausea' and *nauseous* has been used to mean the same in English since at least 1628, while it has been used to mean "nauseated" only since the later 19th century – though it was in use by 1618 to mean 'inclined to nausea; squeamish'.

Still, meanings shift; there are many words that have changed quite completely in meaning over the centuries. And what a word is used for is, ultimately, what it is used for – we can try to enforce specific meanings, but if everyone ignores them and goes with a different meaning, then the language has shifted, which it does all the time. And *nauseous* is now used almost exclusively to mean 'feeling sick'. It is very commonly preceded by *feel*, *feeling*, or *felt*, as well as by *become* and *became*, and may also come with forms of *make*, as in *Today's word tasting note made me nauseous*. Who but the "It is I" crowd would ever say, or expect anyone to understand, *Today's word tasting note was nauseous* to mean the same thing?

pika, pica

"Isn't he cute?"

Elisa Lively was showing us some pictures of a hiking trip in the Rockies. The one at hand was of a round, furry little thing with rounded ears and a small tail. It was playing peek-a-boo behind a rock.

"Is that a pika?" I asked. (I used the anglicized "pie-ca" pronunciation.)

"It doesn't look like a magpie to me," Maury commented.

"Yes! No... what?" Elisa said, first to me, then to Maury, then to space.

"*Pica* is Latin for 'magpie,'" Maury said.

"This is *pika* with a *k*," I said.

"I see," Maury said. Or maybe it was "I '*c*'."

"Wait," said Elisa. "*Pica* with a *c* is like when I used to eat clay when I was a kid."

"A compulsion to eat non-food things," Maury said, "so named because magpies will eat just about anything."

"They could have named it after goats," I noted. "*Caper* or *capra*. If it had been *caper* it might have been especially picaresque. *Capra* seems to me a bit more of a wonderful word, to be frank."

"*Capraphilia?*" Maury said macaronically. "Well, that does sound like a kind of pica. But yuck."

"Pikas do eat their own doo-doo," I mentioned, "like rabbits. They pass everything through twice."

Elisa pulled a face. "That's not why they're called that, though, is it?"

I waved the suggestion away lightly. "No, with a *k* it's from a Siberian language, Evenki."

"Siberia!" Elisa said. "They get around for such little things."

"How big is it, anyway?" Maury gestured at the photo.

"About eight inches, I think," Elisa said. "I didn't place a ruler for scale," she added, a rather dry remark for her.

"A pica ruler?" I quipped.

"About forty-eight picas, by the sound of it," Maury riposted.

Elisa looked at the two of us and then at the photo and appeared to be about to ask for clarification. We didn't wait. "A pica is a measurement of type," I said. "One sixth of an inch. There are twelve points to a pica."

"It was originally a size of type, when they used to refer to type sizes by name," Maury added. "It seems to have been named after an ecclesiastical directory, which was set in type of that size; the directory in turn was probably named after a magpie, and I don't know why. Something to do with its colour and appearance, maybe."

"Well, those magpies do collect," I said, not really expecting the double pun to be appreciated.

"Yes, they're not pikers," Maury tossed in. "Or perhaps they are. And on what pike did you pick this little peeker?"

"It was near Lake Louise," she said, "back towards Skoki Lodge, actually."

"Oh, well, that's suitable," I said. "There's a ski run on the back side of the Lake Louise ski area called *Pika*. You would have passed it on your way to Skoki." I paused and a little lightbulb went on over my head. I grinned. Neither of my interlocutors were ski racing fans but I didn't care. "Lake Louise is also where Picabo Street won her first World Cup downhill victory. She won there the following year, too. Not on Pika, though – that's an easy run."

"Peek-a-boo Street?" Elisa said, her brow furrowing. "What are you talking about?"

"Spelled *P-i-c-a-b-o*," I explained. "The Lindsay Vonn of the mid-nineties."

Elisa and Maury looked at each other for a moment and then Elisa flipped to the next picture. "Now, this is Skoki Lodge," she said. "It's run by this nice guy called Leo Mitzel and his wife, Katie…"

squee

"DUDE," JESS SAID, SETTING her pint down and leaning forward, "let it go. You're harshing the squee."

"I..." I paused. "What?" I glanced at Daryl, who seemed to have understood her.

"You're harshing the squee," Jess repeated. "Don't go pick pick picking at fiction all the time. Willing suspension of disbelief! Sci fi is allegory anyway, so never mind about their needing three years to learn the language after arriving on the planet."

"Harshing the squee." I pulled out my soft leather Letts and my Cross mechanical pencil and wrote it down. "Does that mean what I think it means?"

Daryl reached into the basket and grabbed a sweet potato fry. "It means you're pissing in the popcorn." He dipped the fry and relaxed back with it.

I looked at the two of them. "This is apparently a term I'm supposed to know? It's current? *Squee?*"

Jess smiled. "You're getting old. And out of touch." She stuck her tongue out.

"*Squee* is a noise fangirls make," Daryl said. "You know, anime fangirls, so excitable. It started out as onomatopoeia −" ("An ideophone," Jess interjected) −"and has become a verb and a noun and probably an adjective too somewhere." Ah, yes, the versatility of the English language − and of ideophones, which are words that have a performative aspect to them, like *lickety-split*, *whoosh*, and so on.

"No doubt," I observed, "the fangirls become 'woo girls' once they're old enough to get into bars − those girls who scream, 'Partyyyyyy! Wooooo!'" I sipped my dark pint. "*Squee* is a really nice, expressive word. It has an imitative feel to it, as you say, but also draws on some good current phonaesthemes. It echoes *squeal* and *squeak*, using the /skw/ to intensify the high-pitched /i/, sliding in on the /s/ and then, like a shuffleboard puck, knocking the rest of the word forward with the /kw/."

"And that /i/ by itself," Jess added. "An expression of glee, as in *whee* and *whoopee* and *yee-haw*."

"And there's also the hint of *squeeze* and *squeegee* cut off," I mused. I reached for a sweet potato fry and found I was taking the last one.

"Another reference you're too old to know," Daryl said, "is that *Squee* is also the name of the main character in a comic book series."

"Oh, come now," Jess said. "Surely James has read *Johnny the Homicidal Maniac*."

I looked at them with a slight smile and washed down the rest of my beer.

Daryl was getting busy with his iPhone. After a moment he held it out to me. It was displaying a page from TV Tropes, which turned out to be a treasure trove of citations from popular culture of uses of squee. I scrolled and read. Scroll scroll scroll. "Only tweenage screams of ecstasy have the strength to cut a hole in space itself!" Scroll scroll scroll. I stopped and stared at yet another must-take-out-my-Letts-and-Cross-pencil word. "*Nerdgasm!*" I looked up. "Squee!"

The waitress had just happened by at that very moment. Jess turned to her and said, "He needs another."

The waitress looked at me. "I think I might need to see some ID."

deliquium

I WAS AT ONE of the Order of Logogustation's weekly word tastings and had just been served up *deliquium* when I heard a sound that caused a ripple of horripilation down my spine. It was the unmistakeable creak of matching his-and-hers black leather pants and jackets, and it was right… behind me… looking… over… my… shoulder…

"Mmm, what have we here?" purred Marilyn Frack, 32 millimetres from my ear. "*Deliquium*! Look, Edgar!" Her other half, Edgar Frick, appeared on my other side, peering at the word I held in my hand.

"Well, now, there's a liquid-looking word," declared Edgar.

"In spite of the fact that there's only one liquid in it," I said, meaning the /l/.

"But you see," Marilyn said, "it has two cups, *u u*."

"And two candles, *i i*," Edgar added.

"Well, then," Marilyn said, turning towards Edgar, "it's just you and I, with two cups and two candles! Let us drink deeply!"

"And perhaps," I said, "you'll drink so much you'll pass out. That is, you will suffer deliquium."

"Pass out!" Marilyn said. "Become as liquid and flow to the floor?"

"It's a trick word," I said. "Although there is an obsolete word *deliquium* that means 'deliquescence,' which is melting or becoming liquid by absorbing moisture from the air –"

Marilyn broke into her impression of Katarina Witt in *Battle of the Blades*: "I'm melting in my seat, and I don't mean my armpits!" She smiled and licked her lips.

"I don't think she meant absorption, either," I said. "But while that *deliquium* and the sound of *liquid* have affected the interpretation and use of this word, the sense of swooning or syncope – actually through hypotension rather than intoxication – comes from a Latin homonym meaning 'failure' which is formed from a past tense form of the same Latin root that gives us *delinquent*."

"One of my favourite words," Edgar said, "to embody."

"Then you will commit many a *delict*," I said, "which is an offence against the law, coming to us from the same root by way of *delictum*, which means 'fault', 'offence', 'crime'."

Marilyn's left eyebrow arched archly. "As in *in flagrante delicto*! Oo, now I *could* swoon!"

"We really must thank James for introducing us to this delectable lexeme," Edgar said, leering heavy-lidded past me at his lover.

"*Deliquium?*" Marilyn said, leaning close in on me. "Let's. Do we lick 'im?"

At which point I believe I lost consciousness.

thwack

"SO IT COMES TO HIM," Daryl said, gesturing, "and THWACK!, he just nails it."

I emitted a descending whistle of appreciation in response.

Raoul, interested though he may sometimes be in sports tales, was as usual more interested in the sport of words. "What part of speech is that?"

"What," Daryl asked. "*Nails?*"

"No, *thwack*," Raoul said.

"Well, a *thwack* can be a noun, and *thwack* can be a verb…"

"Yes," Raoul said, "'He thwacked it a good thwack.' But this wasn't either of those, was it? More of an interjection, I think."

"You can interject nouns and verbs," Daryl said. "*Nuts!*" He paused for a split second and then, having thought of it, grabbed some nuts from the bowl on the table. Then he pulled out his iPhone and started typing on it.

"But saying that when you encounter catastrophe is not like saying it when you encounter cashews," Raoul objected. "It's not like saying 'Bees!' or 'Incoming!' or 'Run!' or 'Help!' It's not indexical; it doesn't indicate the presence of, or need for, nuts. Nor do I think *thwack* is like *nuts* – one says *nuts* where one could equally say *drat* or *rats* or any of several less polite things. *Thwack* indicates something more specific. Perhaps one could say *smack* or *whack*, depending on the impression of the sound…"

"Well," Daryl said, flicking through screens on his iPhone, "it's onomatopoeia, and has been with us at least since about 1530, first as a verb and then as a noun. Shakespeare used it in *Coriolanus*. I find no listing for it as an interjection."

"Ah," I said, deciding my time to dive in had come, "the insistent neglect of ideophones. Even in African languages, some of which have hundreds of them and use them fairly often, they were a long time in being recognized and studied. For some reason many linguists don't find them interesting enough to study, which I find truly strange. Things that break the expected patterns and categories are the most fascinating!"

"Ideophones?" said Daryl. Tap tap tap he went on his iPhone.

"A particularly performative set of words. Not per se a lexical category; they can be any other word class. But they add an element of performance, and often have unusual sounds and grammatical aspects."

"Onomatopoeia," said Raoul. "Straightforward imitation."

"Standardized, lexicalized, and not always imitative," I said. "In some languages, for instance, there are ideophones to emphasize intensity of colour – different ones for different colours. Some also use gestures and non-speech sounds. For instance," I increased my level of performative involvement, "'Was he in trouble?'" Onto the end of this, as answer, I tacked a low whistle with eyes wide open and right hand fanning head. Then I added, "And that's culturally standardized."

"But *thwack* is plain imitation," Raoul insisted.

"Why not *thap* or *thwap* or *swapt* or…" I said.

"I notice you use voiceless fricatives on all of them," Raoul pointed out.

"Well, yes," I said, "that makes the difference between *thwack* and *whack* – the clearer sense of something whistling through the air before impact. That is imitative, but why not *fwack*?"

"Sounds vulgar, doesn't it," Raoul said, and reached for the bowl of nuts.

I tried saying *thwack* and *fwack* a few times. "*Thwack* allows a better pucker and release, a kind of oral gesture imitative of an impact."

Daryl had found something more with his web searching. "They're most likely to be used in fairly active, lively, informal narratives, aren't they?"

"That seems obvious enough," Raoul said.

"And often in the narrative present," Daryl continued.

"Is that what you're finding?" I asked. "That seems reasonable. Just as you used it."

"And," Daryl said, scrolling some more, "frequently with exclamation marks, sometimes all caps or italics, and repetition."

"Well," I said, "voilà! There you have it."

"*Voilà*," Raoul said. "And what part of speech would that be here?"

And so it began again.

fungible, fungi

WE WERE SETTING OUT some refreshments at Domus Logogustationis for our monthly Words, Wines, and Whatever tasting event. Maury had paused to scrutinize a piece of truffled Gorgonzola.

"I believe this is a bit mouldy."

I peered over. Elisa, ready to hand, made a funny face. "It's *supposed* to be! It's blue cheese!" she said.

"Yes," said Maury, holding up the offending wedge, "but there is the mould *in* the cheese and the mould *on* the cheese. Moulds are not fungible."

"Ironically," I said.

"Why ironically?" Elisa asked.

"Because they're fungi," Maury said, pronouncing it "fun-jye."

"Fungi?" Elisa said, saying it "fun-guy."

"I am often thought one such, thank you," Maury replied.

Elisa was about to say something, the caught herself and gave Maury a light swat. "Ha ha. But you said 'fun-jye.'"

"Well, yes," said Maury, "I was going with the usual way of saying anglicized Latin terms. We don't, after all, say *fungible* with a velar *g*. Or pretty much any other similar Latin-derived word, except for *fungi*, which has both options available."

"They're fungible," I said.

"*Fungible*," Elisa said, pondering. "That's a fun word. Sounds a bit like *spongeable*."

"Fittingly," said Maury, "since the word *fungus* comes from the same Greek word that gives us *sponge*."

"But fungi aren't sponges," Elisa said.

"Nope," I said, "sponges are part of the animal kingdom. Fungi are their own kingdom."

"So does *fungible* relate to *fungus*?" Elisa asked.

"No," Maury replied, "it's just a coincidence of sound, though it might have been the basis for various Latin puns. Fungible comes from *fungi vice.*" Maury gave the classical pronunciation – like "foonghee weekeh" – and then repeated the term with the old British-style version, like "fun-jye vie-see."

"To take the place of or fill the office of," I translated. "For things that are fudgeable. Break one glass and you can use another similar one in its stead. A dollar is a dollar. And so on. If any item of the type will do, it's fungible."

"*Fungi vice!*" Elisa giggled, saying it like the name of a mushroom cop show. "Maybe we should call the fungi vice squad on this piece of cheese."

"It might gorgonize them," Maury said.

"They might gorge on it," Elisa riposted.

"Hey," I said in a tough-guy voice, "We ain't lookin' for truffle."

"Another kind of fungus," Maury pointed out. "Also not fungible."

"We ought to have mushrooms here to add to the fun, guys!" Elisa said. She tittered a bit at her pun.

"I'm always leery of mushrooms," Maury said.

"Timothy Leary?" I asked.

"His kind of fungus was more ergot than psilocybin, I think," Maury said (ergot is a mould related to LSD), "but it was the latter kind that struck home to me just how fungible fungi aren't. I knew a fellow in my college days –" (I interjected "Mycology?" but Maury continued) "– who wished to procure some of it for hallucinatory adventures, but he found it unavailable. Someone he knew said he could get him some *Amanita muscaria* instead, another mushroom for trips. Unfortunately, the *Amanita* he got was *phalloides.*"

"Ooo," I said.

"Fotunately for him," Maury continued, "he realized soon enough that he wasn't tripping, and so he took a trip instead to the emergency ward. Saved his life. If he had waited until he had developed cramps a couple of days later, he would likely have died of liver failure within the week."

We paused. Then looked at the truffled Gorgonzola. There was indeed a small spot of surface mold. "Keep or toss, then?" I asked.

Maury took a cheese knife and sliced off the offending part, then placed the rest on the tray. "It won't kill us."

crazy, insane

THE DARYL-AND-MARGOT SHOW WAS at it again, back at the table in the food court overlooking Yonge Street.

"Here," Daryl said, proffering an article from the *New York Times* on his iPhone. "This is emblematic. New York Assemblyman Keith Wright, speaking of the chaos in the state government in Albany, says 'Our forefathers in their infinite wisdom planned for crazy. But this week we moved to insane.'"

"But that's just nonsense!" Margot protested. "He's simply inarticulate. Obviously *crazy* and *insane* mean the same thing exactly. One is simply a more colloquial, less respectful version of the other."

"You mean," I interjected, "one's from Anglo-Saxon and one's from Latin."

"You're crazy," Daryl said (in Margot's direction). "Or perhaps insane. But above all you're inattentive."

"I do not take my lead from the myriad of popular abuses," Margot replied.

"Riiight. And you're the only one in the orchestra who's not off beat," Daryl said. "Meaning is by common agreement, forged through usage. And these two have different usage patterns."

Margot was rummaging through her bag. Evidently she had been tutoring someone who was learning English as a foreign language, as she had the *Oxford Collocations Dictionary* with her. She flipped a few pages and read out. "*Crazy*: *be, seem, sound; go; drive somebody; really, absolutely, completely, totally*…" The she flipped some more. "*Insane*: *be, look, become, go; drive; certify somebody, declare somebody; completely, totally*…" She looked up. "The main difference is that there are technical uses with *insane*: *certify, declare*, also *criminally, clinically*, et cetera."

"So it's OK to say *insane like a fox*?" Daryl asked with a disingenuous smile.

"That's a cliché," Margot replied. "You can't just play around with clichés."

"Clichés give words flavour," I said. "As do popular titles and other common uses."

Daryl had been pulling up some web results on his iPhone while Margot had been rummaging. "Like *Crazy Train*," he said, "*Crazy Horse, Crazy for You, crazy quilt, crazy eights, a wild and crazy guy, dig that crazy cat, man dat some crazy sh—*"

Margot cut him off. "Yes, but those all could have been *insane* except for matters of euphony and formality."

"*Insane Train?*" I chuckled.

"*Insane for You?*" Daryl added, arching an eyebrow. "*Insane eights?*"

"There's no question," I said, "that *crazy* is less formal. After all, aside from being Anglo-Saxon, it originally meant 'cracked.' We still talk about crazing in pottery and glasses. There's even a French cognate, *écraser* – a gift from the Normans, who knew crazy. But the point is that the greater formality and clinicality give *insane* a tone of respect, or awe, or fear, that also gives it a greater degree of severity if one puts one word against the other."

"*Insane* is also unhealthy," Daryl said. "Latin *in* 'not' plus *sanus* 'healthy.' And…" He was tapping on his iPhone as he spoke: "*insane asylum, insane rage… Insane Clown Posse!*"

"As opposed to *crazy clown*, which is what *that coyote is really*," I said. At long last all those Saturday mornings of cartoons were paying off. "The coyote isn't dangerous. Is *dangerously insane* in your collocations dictionary?"

Margot flipped back. "…Yes… But that's because law enforcement officials don't use the word *crazy*, I'd say."

"Right, *insane* is trouble with the law, whereas *crazy* is not; it's just stressful." I abruptly burst into a Billy Joel rendition: "You may be right, I may be crazy, but it just may be a lunatic you're looking for…"

Margot waved her hand as though to dispel smoke. "OK, fine, never mind, stop. You're driving me nuts."

Daryl and I looked at each other and smiled.

"*Nuts*. Lesser degree than crazy?" I said.

"Yes, I think so…" Daryl said.

Margot winced. "My afternoon headache has arrived."

mentor

"WELL," I SAID TO young Marcus Brattle with a touch of trepidation, "I am to be your mentor." I picked up the cup of tea his mother had poured for me just before she disapparated to another part of the house.

Marcus, relishing the lankiness of early adolescence, had strewn himself along and across the chesterfield, a bottle of Coke in arm's reach. "Mum wants to ce*ment our* relationship, does she? Tell me, are you to be com*mentor*, imple*mentor*, or tor*mentor*?"

The last role's likely yours, I thought. I looked around to see if his mother seemed to be anywhere in earshot, and saw no evidence. "Think of me as just the sort of bad influence you need," I said.

"A dementor, then," he said then, almost looking interested. "But is that what you *meant, or…*"

"Well, more like staving off dementia, now that demention it. Not to worry; you are no hirsute ceramicist, and I will not eat your soul. No, you are to play the part of Telemachus."

"Who's he?"

"The student of Mentor. From the *Odyssey*. And, more recently, the lead character in Mothe-Fénelon's 1699 book *Les Aventures de Télémaque*, from which the persona of Mentor came to be popularly known. Our word came up as a reference as much to that book as to the *Odyssey*."

"And here I thought it had to do with mental," Marcus said. "If you're no good, like, that would make me mentor-ly handicapped."

"Well, there is a sense of mentation, " I said, and thought, Probably a little mentition (lying) too, as occasion demands.

"So who was this Telemetry bloke, anyway?"

"The son of Odysseus and Penelope. No doubt you've read James Joyce's *Ulysses*," I said, hoping that he certainly had not, because after all he was only in grade 9. "Stephen Dedalus was the Telemachus type in that. In the *Odyssey*, Mentor was Telemachus's tutor, but actually Mentor was Athena in disguise."

"Athena!" Marcus got up and dumped himself into a chair at the table, setting his Coke next to my tea. "Athena was a female. (I think I knew a girl called Athena…) Are you saying this Mentor was really a Womentor?"

"Better that than a Minotaur, anyway."

"Oh, with a nice girl, you always want more than a minotaur two," Marcus said, and had a slug of his Coke. "So what you're saying is that *mentee* is not a real word."

"It's a real word," I said, "because people use it and understand it, but it's a backformation. Like *tase* from *Taser*."

"Shocking. So you're the minotaur and I'm the manatee. Oh, the huge manatee!" He threw his arms in the air in mock tragedy.

"Well, at least you'll have mentee-fresh breath," I said.

This seemed to provoke a recollection of something; Marcus started checking his pockets. As he did so, he asked, "And where, then, did this name *Mentor* come from?"

"It seems it came from the Greek word for 'intent, spirit, purpose, action,' that sort of thing: *mentos*."

"Marvellous!" Marcus said with an evil little smile, producing something from his pocket that I only too late identified as a roll of Mentos. Before I could stop him, he emptied it into his still-mostly-full bottle of Coke. A geyser of foam shot towards the ceiling. As it drenched me and my tea, he shouted, "A fountain of knowledge!"

flutterbudget

I WAS GIVING A CLASS in word tasting, and from a book by L. Frank Baum I had pulled a real winner – not only a flavourful word that trips a pretty fillip on the tongue, but one signifying something that could well use a word like this to signify it. I wrote it on the blackboard: *flutterbudget*.

I turned to the class. "Let's all say this together."

Most of those in attendance obliged, if perfunctorily. One hand shot up. I quickly glanced at my diagram of who was sitting where. "Yes, Eleanor?"

"I don't think we should say that."

I blinked. "Well, why not?"

"It just sounds vulgar."

I was momentarily taken aback – as were, from what I could tell, most of the others in the class. "It's not vulgar," I said. "It doesn't mean anything vulgar. If it were vulgar, you would know it. And we can't have phonetic profiling. There's no value in avoiding words just because they sound like something bad. You'd cross out a huge portion of the English vocabulary. …Although I can't really think exactly what vulgar thing you think this sounds like, aside from its starting with *f* and having an 'uh' sound in it."

"If we said this on the street," Eleanor protested, "someone might think we were saying something rude."

"They might think that no matter what you say if they don't understand it," I said, and noticed another hand up. "Brian?"

"I think it sounds like *flibbertigibbet*," Brian said. "Or… *butterfly*."

"*Fussbudget*," piped up a voice from the back that I determined was Anna.

I put one finger on the tip of my nose and pointed the other at her. "Bingo. Same budget. Slightly different sense."

Another hand, at the back. I glanced quickly… "Kayley?"

"A fussbudget is someone who worries about money a lot, right?" Kayley asked.

"Just someone who fusses a lot," I said. "Someone who finds fault and makes fusses all the time. A nitpicker. The *budget* is not our most common sense now but the sense that it grew out of. Just as *bank* comes from a table for handling money, *budget* comes from a purse for storing it in. It's from French *bougette*, diminutive of *bouge*, which means 'bag' and also gave us *bulge* – so if the bulge in your pocket is a wallet, then it's perfectly apposite. Anyway, from the bag sense came the contents sense – a budget can still be a bundle, the contents of a wallet or sock. Now picture that being a bunch of fusses."

"Or flutters!" Anna interjected from the back.

"Well, it's not right," Eleanor said. "Talking about fluttering budgets just invites trouble."

"Because a budgie might flutter away with your money?" Anna chirped.

"You don't want to talk about losing money," Eleanor said primly.

"Well, this doesn't," I said. "The flutters here are needless worries – butterflies in the stomach, what-ifs. The word is from L. Frank Baum's *The Emerald City of Oz* – the Flutterbudgets are a group of people who spend all their time worrying about things that could happen or that might have happened but didn't. Their favourite word is *if*. For example, one of them has pricked her finger with a needle." Eleanor winced, whether at *pricked* or at the description of violence I'm not sure. "She is terribly afraid that she will get blood poisoning. Dorothy tells her that she – Dorothy – has pricked her finger many times and survived. At first the woman is relieved, but then she starts wailing again: 'Oh, suppose I had pricked my foot! Then the doctors would have cut my foot off, and I'd be lamed for life!' And so on."

"I'd rather be a flibbertigibbet." Of course that was Anna.

"It's not nice to make fun of people who are concerned," Eleanor said.

"There are the concerned," I said, "and then there are the worrywarts and hand-wringers. Anyway, we are here to taste words. And this one trips around nicely on the lips, the tip of the tongue, the teeth, with just one retroflex. ...Brian?"

"In a British pronunciation there wouldn't be the retroflex *r*," Brian said. "There would be three of basically the same vowel, three syllables in a row."

"True, more or less," I said, "but we're Canadian, and Baum was American, so we and he get the alternating pattern. We all get the nice, bouncy four syllables, though. There are quite a few words with that kind of double trochee, all the way from *pitter-patter* and *fuddy-duddy* to *paternoster*."

"That's sacrilegious!" Eleanor exclaimed.

I was about to respond to that, but at the same time, from the back of the class, the voice of Anna chimed in, "Or *motherf—*"

I very nearly leapt across the room, but Kayley saved me the trouble, clapping her hand over Anna's mouth.

Eleanor's eyes widened accusingly as she looked at me over her glasses. "What if someone had been here? What would they think?"

kitsch

A GASP OF HORROR with the vocal catch of retching issued forth from the kitchen of Domus Logogustationis, the headquarters of the Order of Logogustation. I recognized Maury's voice of dismay right away and went to have a look-see. There, in the kitchen, over a hutch, hung a diptych: a cricket match of fluffy kittens, and a poker game of puppies with bows on their heads.

"Who put the kitsch in the kitchen?!" Maury moaned, twitching.

"Which kitsch," I said, unable to resist a chance to twist Maury's knickers, "the kitten kitsch or the bitch kitsch?"

"Each. Both. Whatever! I know we're not rich, but this gives me an itch – to pitch it in a ditch!"

"But it fills out this niche. Maybe adjust them a titch…"

Maury turned to look at me. "You didn't do this, did you?"

"Oh, no," I said, actually shivering a bit at the thought. "Perhaps they were picked up at Elisa's kaffeeklatsch. Well, at least they match."

Maury peered at them over the tops of his glasses – either for expressive effect, or just to see them less clearly; he's unmistakeably myopic. "Kittens on a cricket pitch," he said slowly. "I'd rather dispatch it down the coney hatch. The mutts, too. The worst sort of kitsch. Vulgar. Sentimental. Sickeningly saccharine. Wretched."

"It's funny," I mused, "that something so invariably soapy, smeary, or fluffy as kitsch gets an unfluffy, unsoapy, unsmeary word like *kitsch*. I think our conversation has established how basically harsh and unpleasant that voiceless affricate is for a word ending. And the onset is the hardest phoneme going in English, /k/."

"Ironic to say it's unsmeary," said Maury, "given that it comes from dialectal German *kitschen*, verb, 'smear'."

"Well, one does smear things in the kitchen," I said.

"I'd rather have cockroach caca than this botch job. I mean," he said, gesturing at the dog picture, "this one has taken archetypical schlock – C.M. Coolidge's 1903 poker-playing dog series – and spatch-cocked it with saccharine. The originals were done to sell cigars. These are not for the cigar crowd!"

"Curiously," I said, "*kitsch* is only attested in English since the 1920s, if I recall correctly. …The word, I mean, of course. We've had the thing for much longer. Along with the words *maudlin, mawkish, cloying,* and *tawdry.*"

"Well, who knows what made *kitsch* catch on just then," Maury said. He stepped forward, unhitched the kitten picture, and stood there for a moment, holding it, looking for a good place to stick it. "Hand me that butcher knife," he said.

But just then Elisa came in. "Ah-ah-ahhh!" she sang, and snatched the picture from Maury. "Don't touch!"

"You can't be serious," Maury said in a wounded voice as she replaced the picture.

"Oh," Elisa chirped, "they won't stay there forever. They're on loan from my aunt. They're just theme decoration for our upcoming vulgarity week."

"Ross Ewage will oblige quite readily at the sight of these," Maury rumbled.

"Kittens and vulgarity…" I smiled. "Never mind kitsch. Try Joel Veitch!" I went grabbed a slip of paper and wrote down a link for her. "No kitsch there… but plenty of the other, unsentimental kind of vulgarity. And lots of kittens. If you don't like the vulgar, you might want to skip the sweary kittens. And a few other things."

skirl

"IT'S NO A *SKIRT*!"

Philip McCarr leapt to his feet, which were a fair ways down. He was not referring to his kilt, for once; the hapless Arthur Watkins had misread Philip's entry for the word tasting. "It's *skirl*, man!"

Arthur was slightly taken aback and tried to make sense of this. "A... it's a girl with a skirt?"

Philip's naturally red colour saturated a bit more. "It's no *girl* and no *skirt*, it's *skirl*! Th' soond th' bagpipes make!" He turned to the room and declaimed what at first sounded like a rather nasty imprecation but in fact was a descriptive passage from Robert Burns's "Tam o' Shanter": "He screw'd the pipes and gart them skirl, Till roof and rafters a' did dirl." He paused thoughtfully for a moment and said, "Nice word, that, *dirl*. Cognate wi' thrill. Same meanin', like, or 'to ring or vibrate'."

Arthur was still confused for a moment. "I'm sorry, I... Oh, *s-k-i-r-l*. Yes of course. What bagpipes do."

Philip threw his hands up. "Theeeeere y'have it, man." He dropped himself back into his chair and tended to his vocal cords with a glass of Scotch.

"A shrill sound," said Montgomery Starling-Byrd. "Or, as a verb, to make a shrill sound."

"Ah wonder," interjected the gathering's southern belle, Grace Sherman, "whethah *shrill* and *skirl* are cognate."

Montgomery angled his head back towards her. "One might suspect it, given that an earlier form of *skirl* is *skrill*, and it came from Scandinavian, and *sk* before a high front vowel has in modern Swedish and Norwegian become a palatal fricative. But *shrill* is traced to German, and research does not go past that on this one."

"You know, I'm sure, tha ither meaning," Philip said to Montgomery, and I had the sense he was hoping Montgomery did not.

"Another meaning?" Montgomery said. "I'm sure I don't use it enough even for one meaning." He smiled pleasantly. Montgomery could never gladly give a Scotsman the upper hand.

"My quote fra 'Tam o' Shanter' wis relevant tae this as weel," Philip said. "For 'twas auld Nick himself blowing the pipes, and wee witchies dancing a twirl and casting off their duddies till they were ainley in their sarks."

"Chemises," I gamely translated, not sarcastically.

"And tae fly wi' a sweeping or swirling motion – weel, th' birds may do it, but so may a sark. And that, too, is to skirl. Different word, tho."

"So," said Grace, getting up gracefully, "if a girl's skirt and shirt made a twirl or a swirl like a school of krill" – she began to swing and swirl her flowing garments – "and in the skirl caught a curl and hurled free" – she spun faster and threw off her shawl – "then the girl might skirl, too." Which Grace immediately did – she let out a short shriek, which it soon became evident was actually involuntary: along with her shawl, she had lost her blouse and her footing, and she landed squarely in Philip's lap.

Philip looked down at her with an approving smile and toasted her with his glass of Scotch. "Weel done, Cutty-sark!"

tempura

"O TEMPURA! O MORASS!" Maury fumed, standing over some soggy shrimp fritters in his kitchen.

"O temper! O Maury!" I replied, coming over to look. "I take it the temperature was insufficient?"

"First there was the intemperately tamped tempeh, and now this trumps it! Deux fois trompé!"

"Trempette de foie?" I said, proffering pâté.

Maury dabbed a chip in it. "My culinary self-esteem is taking a dip." He wandered into his living room and dropped himself into a chair.

"You're just gaining seasoning," I said, following him.

"Like a frying pan. I might as well have stuck with painting." He gestured at a tempera of a temple. "Rather Apollo than appalling."

"Where is that?"

"The Vale of Tempe, Greece." He declaimed the beginning of Keats's "Ode on a Grecian Urn":

"Thou still unravish'd bride of quietness,
Thou foster-child of Silence and slow Time,
Sylvan historian, who canst thus express
A flowery tale more sweetly than our rhyme:
What leaf-fringed legend haunts about thy shape
Of deities or mortals, or of both,
In Tempe or the dales of Arcady?
What men or gods are these? What maidens loth?
What mad pursuit? What struggle to escape?
What pipes and timbrels? What wild ecstasy?"

"Et in arcadia ego," I said. "Beats its namesake Tempe, Arizona, anyway."

"Where you can fry an egg on the sidewalk," Maury said. His testiness tempered, he rose again and returned to the kitchen.

"Well," I said, "your food's not so unlike painting. Egg tempura and oil. It's the same root, anyway, *tempura* and *tempera*."

"For which we can thank those Portuguese missionaries to Japan of four centuries ago. Them and their *tempuras*, which were meat-free days."

"Other sources say it comes from *tempêro*, 'seasoning,'" I pointed out. "It's a tasting kind of word, anyway, tip and lip, like *dip* – French *trempette*. Anyway, *temper, tempera, temperature, tempura*, all trace back to *temperare*, 'divide in due portion', 'mingle', 'temper', 'exercise restraint'…"

"Whereas *tempeh* comes from Indonesian." Maury stood over his counter again and contemplated his ingredients. Seeing that the oil had heated up somewhat, he began dipping vegetables into the batter. "Well, I might as well view this as just a temporary setback. No point in dumping it just because it's a bit damp." He glanced up at the clock. "Tempus fugit!"

trifle

OTHER ORGANIZATIONS HAVE CAKE SALES or bake sales or similar events. At the Order of Logogustation we're just a little more paronomastic in our purveyance for mastication. This fact was gradually dawning on one of the visitors to our little sale, who was finding at every table nothing but variations on the same theme: a layered dessert, with a base of sponge cake or Swiss rolls soaking in peach juice and sherry, fruit and fruit-flavoured jelly next, then custard, and whipped cream on top.

"Lovely desserts," said the gentleman, finishing his fourth bowl, "but it's a bit odd that it's all versions of the same dessert."

"A bit odd?" said Maury. "A trifle bizarre, I'd say."

He pointed at the sign hanging at the back of the room, which read *A Trifle Bazaar.*

The gentleman arched his left eyebrow, then peered at it again over his glasses, presumably so that he would not have to see it in focus. He made a sally of his own. "You're trifling with me."

Philippe, at an adjoining table, leaned forward and said, "Would you like to try fol another one? Mine is marked with a trefoil." He displayed a three-ring shape.

"That could be trouble," the gentleman said.

"Foiled again," Philippe replied.

"At least you didn't make it with truffles," Maury noted.

Philippe was unruffled. "I was going to use the chocolate kind, not the fungus."

Jess joined in from the other side. "Deviation is not brooked. No trufflemakers here. Trifles are very tribal."

"So," the gentleman said, "are you getting much traffic?"

"There may be later, when we have the raffle," Jess said. "Then there may be a kerfuffle."

"There was one last year," Maury said, "because there was a mix-up. The winner took home not a trifle but a *lifter*."

"Went home," Jess said, "had some *t*, and came back with a *rifle*."

Philippe rejoined. "I thought it was a *filter* that was won."

"You don't seem to have much in the way of filters around here," the gentleman observed. "The language is open to an *e flirt*."

Everyone paused and looked at him. They were all thinking that the Order of Logogustation could suit him to a *t* – he could become a *lifer*.

"But surely you are not saying," he continued, "that *truffle, trefoil*, et cetera are all related to *trifle*."

"Naturally not," Philippe said. "We just jest."

Maury explained. "*Trifle* comes from *trufa*, Spanish, 'jest, leer', or *truffa*, Italian, 'cheat, con'. Now, however, although it is on the books as meaning 'an insignificant thing', the great majority of its use is as an indefinite quantifier. Like *a bit*, only fancier."

"Well," said the gentleman, stepping over to Philippe's table, "that seems fitting enough, as I fancy a bit more."

however

MONTGOMERY STARLING-BYRD, LATELY ELECTED Grand Panjandrum of the Order of Logogustation, was in town and made a stop by our local Domus Logogustationis for the monthly Words, Wines, and Whatever tasting event. We took this as a chance to generate a little extra interest and invited various parties to come be addressed. And so Montgomery stood in the middle of our Rather Good Hall (not quite up to the level of a Great Hall) surrounded by students, journalists, and student journalists, and gave a rousing and mercifully brief discourse on why English should be viewed as a game, and not one with tightly fixed rules, either. He then entertained questions.

One young fellow in a red shirt piped up: "Why does the name of your society mix Latin and Greek? Doesn't that seem a little sloppy?"

Montgomery arched an eyebrow slightly. "It's hardly the first macaronic word in the language. In fact, we mixed *logo* and *gustation* partly as an expression of the sort of play I was just speaking of. It's true that a more cleanly Latin formation would be *verbogustation*. However, that would have far too strong a taste of *bogus*."

The assembled scribes scribbled. One said to her friend next to her, "Comma with the *however*?"

Red shirt looked back over his shoulder. "Never!"

A green-shirted young woman said, "What do you mean, never? Always!"

"No," said a slip of a thing in a black dress, "a period."

"A period?!" said the first. "Oh... no, I meant after."

"Not a period!" said red shirt. "Always a semicolon. One should not start a sentence with a conjunctive adverb."

Montgomery's eyebrow raised a titch more. Before he could interject, the first woman's friend, a girl in a pink button-up, said, "People don't speak with semicolons. Didn't you learn that? Any journalism professor will tell you that."

"I speak with semicolons," Montgomery interjected. "And I believe some journalism professors do as well. However, in this instance, I intended *however* to be the start of a new sentence."

"Boy," said red shirt, "you really are a lot of descriptivists, aren't you? Throwing Strunk and White out the window?"

Maury, in the background, had anticipated this, and had plucked a copy of the very book off the shelf. He handed it to Montgomery open to page 43. Montgomery read aloud: "Avoid starting a sentence with *however* when the meaning is 'nevertheless.' The word usually serves better when not in first position." He handed the book back to Maury. "Two observations: first, even were Strunk and White holy writ, which it certainly is not, that is a recommendation, not an absolute rule; second, as just mentioned, it is not holy writ. It is opinion. And whoever told you never to start a sentence with *however* is terribly misguided."

"We need rules," protested red shirt.

"We have rules," Montgomery said. "Otherwise me to able you understand wouldn't be."

A chorus of "What?" broke out.

"Exactly," said Montgomery. "Now, let's see what you all have for the disputed phrase. However you may have it, it is likely to be understood; however, you may have it in a way that transgresses the expected norms of standard English."

Those assembled surveyed their transcriptions. Aside from assorted other errors and inaccuracies, the following renditions were found:

...verbugustation, however that would have...
...verbogustation, however, that would have...
...verbogustation however, that would have...
...verbogustation. However that would have...
...verbogustation; however that would have...
...verbogustation; however, that would have...
...verbogustation. However, that would have...

"Formally," Montgomery said, "only these last two are correct, and it is the last which I intended. Conjunctive adverbs are offset from their clauses with commas. If they come first in a clause, the preceding clause boundary is marked with a period or semicolon, as always. A *however* without commas setting it off is the other *however*." Montgomery paused for the briefest of moments. "Which, however," he added, "is the same *however*. It is simply differently used."

Several of the scribblers were darting their eyes around at their friends to see if they had successfully parsed Montgomery's latest utterance.

Montgomery continued, warming to the subject. "The *ever* – which, incidentally, is as etymologically puzzling as *dog* – is attached to *wh*-words to give them a sort of generalized, indefinite force: *whoever said whatever whenever wherever however*. (There may seem to be no *whyever*, but whyever shouldn't there be?) As a conjunctive adverb, *however* is shortened from *however this may be*, which is why we treat it as a dependent clause. We see a similar shortening, for instance, in the use of *as far as*: whereas formerly all would say *as far as 'however' goes*, now many will say simply *as far as 'however'*. Goes to show, doesn't it?"

Montgomery smiled slightly and gave his little round button of office a tweak. "Clearly there is some confusion over this word; faced with it, *we hover* between certainty and despair, and know not *how* to *veer*. But let its form serve as a mnemonic to you: just as it has a *w* and then a *v*, you may think of it as having a single mark – a comma – after, and a double mark – a semicolon – before, or a double-strength pause – a period. Then your usage will not change as the weather."

Another pause. Most of those who had been writing were no longer certain whether to write or not.

"However," Montgomery added, "those are the formal rules, required of editors; linguists have the luxury of simply observing the variations. And in the Order of Logogustation we usually hew slightly more to the linguist's side, with a healthy dose of fun tossed in." He smiled. "Are we having fun yet?"

Red shirt, stuffing his materials in his bag, looked up. "Whatever."

toilet

My WORD TASTING CLASS was reconvening after a brief intermission. "Well," I said, "now that we're all back from our toilet…"

Eleanor, near the front, immediately shot her hand up, and proceeded without waiting for acknowledgement: "Please don't be vulgar."

Here we go again. "Vulgar?" I arched my left eyebrow.

"Graphic. You seem to revel in the foul. There is no need to assail us with such indelicate images."

The right eyebrow joined the left. "You find my reference to a lace doily foul?"

"You said *doily*?" Eleanor knitted her brows. "It sounded like something else."

"*Toilet*," I said. "A word that originally referred to a little piece of fabric that was used to cover a woman's dressing-table. From French *toilette*, related to *toile*, 'fabric'. The same *toile* also came to English as *toil*, a now-uncommon word for a net for catching game. Of course, I'm being disingenuous; no one uses *toilet* to mean 'fabric' now. But, really, it is interesting that you find it so unacceptably graphic when it was originally intended as a euphemism. *Washroom* and its Latin-based equivalent *lavatory* are more literal, even if more polite-sounding to us now."

Anna piped up from the back of the room. "Maybe *crapper* would be better."

Kayley, next to Anna, raised her hand. "You know that's from the inventor of the flush toilet, John Crapper."

I was about to speak when Brian saved me the effort; he turned back to Kayley and said, "Too perfect to be true. Actually, though Thomas Crapper, the 19th-century British plumbing company owner, did make flush toilets, he didn't invent them, and the word *crap* is much older."

"Thank you, Brian," I said, "you're quite correct. The word *crap* has been in English to refer to waste since the middle ages. Michael Quinion has a very good run-down of the term and its relation to Thomas Crapper on his site, worldwidewords.org. And commodes have a long developmental history that was certainly added to, but certainly not started, by Thomas Crapper."

"But it's in Trivial Pursuit!" Kayley protested.

I shrugged. "I know. Their research was not quite good enough on this one. It happens."

Eleanor was sitting with her face puckered as though she was sucking on a bitter lemon, shaking her head. "It's indecent," she said to the fellow sitting next to her, a skinny, beleaguered sort named Rupert. "And I fail to see the connection between lace and lavatories."

"Lace and lavatories!" I said. "Well, thereby hangs a tale."

Anna, at the back, sang, "Give to me your lavatory, take from me my lace." Ah, Stevie Nicks. At least she didn't make a comment on hanging tails.

"A woman's dressing-table came to be referred to as her *toilette*," I said. "We still see that in some usages. *Eau de toilette*, which is a version of perfume. *Toilet soap*, an old term for face soap and hand soap."

Brian raised his hand. "There are many paintings with title such as 'Lady So-and-So at Her Toilet,' and they're getting dressed or doing their hair."

"You can get pictures with titles like that now on the web," Anna said, "but they're not getting dressed…" Kayley stifled a giggle. Eleanor turned and glared at Anna.

"The point," I said, "is that the dressing-table was the toilet, and then *toilet* came to refer to the action of dressing, or washing and grooming, and to the room in which that was done. And then, out of delicacy, the fixture came to be referred to using the same word. And now the table has turned. We take the word *toilet* to be a literal word for the fixture. But, now, what do you think is the relation of the sound of the word to its developed sense?"

Rupert raised his hand. "Yes, Rupert?" I said, almost surprised.

"Well, sometimes you have to *toil at* what you're doing there…"

Eleanor pulled a face as though someone had just held a fresh dog turd under her nose.

I laughed just a little. "True, sometimes. But is the 'oy' sound a contributor to the sense of indelicacy of this word? I mean, *oily* is not so nice, but *doily* is fine. *Boil* is somewhat neutral with a little negative shading. *Boy* is fine; *goy* – well, all that Yiddish *oy* has its own flavour which will probably vary somewhat by hearer. It also relates to the Brooklyn-style 'oi' kind of sound for syllabic /r/, as in 'boid' for *bird*, 'goil' for *girl*, and so on, all of which has a lower-class connotation."

Brian raised his hand. "Hypercorrection from that has given us pronunciations such as 'ersters' and 'terlet'."

"Indeed," I said. "Does it have the same feel to say 'terlet'? Or to say it in the French style, 'twa-let'?"

"French is much more elegant," Kayley offered from the back.

"It tends to have that connotation, because of cultural images we have acquired, and the high-toned context of usage of French terms in English," I said. "French itself has its highs and lows, and I don't know whether I would call a language with so many inefficiencies elegant structurally – but that's a more mathematical use of *elegant*. Anyway, French may get moved in a different direction thanks to less rarefied words such as *poutine*."

"That would be a good word for *toilet!*" Anna declared. "*Poo-tine!* Like a canteen for poo!"

"Can you please stop!" Eleanor's shout of disgust was taking on the pleading air of the delicate stomach.

"To return to the 'oi' sound," I said, hoping to calm things down a little, "does it suggest a shape to you?"

Rupert raised his hand again. I looked at him. He waited for me to say something. "Yes, Rupert?"

"I think it's like a spring, 'boing boing boyoyoyoyyy,' so I think it's like a spiral."

Brian smiled a little. "Like water swirling in the bowl."

Kayley raised her hand. "Did you know that it swirls the other way in Australia?"

Brian was about to respond, but I beat him to it this time. "Actually, the direction of the swirl is really determined in the main by the positioning of the water jets."

"But it's like the bathtub drain," Kayley said. "It's the coriolanus effect."

"Coriolis," I said simultaneously with Brian, but we were both drowned out by Anna, who declared triumphantly, "Corral your anus!"

Eleanor was alternating between white and red. She stood and said, "Excuse me. I need to be excused. I require... to be excused. To go down the hall." She rushed out, words failing her.

Rupert looked at her retreating form and smiled slightly. Without raising his hand, he said, "She has been caught in our toil."

chum

HEADING TOWARDS THE KITCHEN in Domus Logogustationis, I spied Maury sitting with his head in his hands. "Why so glum, chum?"

Maury looked up. Actually, he looked rather down, but he looked up at me when I spoke.

"I had an old chum for lunch."

Normally I would launch into the obvious pun, but Maury looked like such a chump, I let it slide. "An old school chum?"

"Oh, I think this chum was old school, yes, probably. Whatever school it belonged to would have been rather old, I'm sure."

Pause. "I... You what?" I looked again at Maury, and realized that he looked perhaps a little more peaked than piqued. "Oh. Some dodgy salmon?"

"I am wondering," Maury said, "whether, when the menu said *chum*, it actually meant fish refuse, shark bait."

"Well, where did you have it?"

"The Spa Diner."

"Oh, yes, west on Queens Quay, isn't it. I ate there once. The staff seemed friendly."

"Oh," Maury said wanly, "my waiter was certainly chumming around. It actually seemed a bit much as a chumbled my chunks of chum." (*Chumble* means "nibble" or perhaps "munch" – Maury did not say *chunder*, but he looked as though that might be next.) "The atmosphere was less than elegant. They had CHUM on the radio." (That's a venerable Toronto hit radio station.)

"You should have gone to the Cambodian place," I said. "Then you might have heard Chum Ngek." (A master of Cambodian classical music.)

"And not eaten yecchy chum neck." Maury pulled a little face and looked a whiter shade of pale. "An evil coincidence it was that a nice food fish came to have the same name as a rather variegated mess of fish trash."

"Coincidence indeed," I said, "especially given that chum meaning 'fish refuse' or 'shark bait' may have come from Scots *chum* meaning 'food', while *chum* meaning 'spotted salmon' comes from a Chinook word meaning 'spotted' or 'variegated'."

"At least I didn't eat an old chamber-mate," Maury said, adverting to the origin of the *chum* that means 'friend'.

"Well," I said, turning towards the fridge, wherein a bottle of fizzy awaited my attention, "would you like some champers?"

Maury made a faint wave. "In a bit, perhaps. At the moment I have a chummy ache."

drupe

"DRUPE?" MARICA SAID, PROFFERING a bowl of cherries to her husband, Ronald.

Ronald sighed. "It's the pits."

"Oh, come now, a couple of little stones can't cause so much trouble."

"Not so much the stones as the stem, of course..." Ronald mumbled.

"But who doesn't like a cherry?" Marica insisted.

"Cherry!" Ronald snorted. "It's been years since..." He looked up and focused on the bowl. "Wait. What are we talking about?"

Marica looked at him over the rim of her glasses. "Fruit."

"I'm not sure how to take that," Ronald said.

Marica thrust the bowl into his hands, then took one cherry from it and dropped it in her mouth. Two brief chews and she spat the pit expertly into a garbage can with a "ping"; a bit more closed-mouth action and she stuck out her tongue with a knotted stem. She took it off her tongue and tucked it into Ronald's shirt pocket. "Knots to you," she said. She turned and went over to the bar, leaving Ronald in his usual state of disjuncture, looking like a dupe.

Having observed at a distance, I came over to Ronald. "Marshalling the drupes?" I said. His face started to muster an outraged and confused look, so I pointed at the bowl. "Cherries are drupes. *D-r-u-p-e.* A fruit with a single hard stone in the middle. The exocarp, or skin, encloses a mesocarp, the flesh that we eat, in the middle of which is an endocarp, which is the actual seed. Apricots, cherries, peaches, plums, mangoes, all are drupes."

"Oh," Ronald said. "I'm not sure I got all of that..."

"You got olive," I said. "That's for sure. Overripe olive, to be precise. That's what the Latin term *druppa* originally meant; it was taken from a Greek word for 'olive', which may have been formed from roots meaning 'tree' and 'ripe'."

Pause. "You know," Ronald said, beginning to droop visibly, "I just come to these word tasting things because of Marica." He looked around for a table and saw none nearby, so he held the bowl out to me. "Mind if I drop these on you? I think I want to go get stoned." Pause. "Ha ha," he added drily, and walked off towards Marica.

Maury happened by just then. I held out the bowl. "Drupe?"

"Don't start," Maury said. "I don't mean to be a prude, but I'm not feeling very cherry. I mean cheery."

my bad

MARGOT SIPPED HER LATTE and grimaced. "I wanted it made with non-fat milk!" she protested.

"Whoops," Daryl said, pulling his own from the tray he had just brought. "My bad."

Margot grimaced even more. "Your *bad*? Why can you not speak good English and say *my fault* or *my error*?"

"Since when is *bad* bad English?" I said with feigned innocence.

"If anything," Jess said, playing along, "it's gotten better. Aside from its positively toned colloquial use in African-American Vernacular English, its presence in English seems to stem from an original word *bæddel* referring to a hermaphrodite or effeminate male. Leaving aside the fact that that is the exact opposite of the modern slang sense I just mentioned, it's not very heartening to think that such people were the subject of such opprobrium that they became the byword for poor quality. So much better to see this word and its original subjects separated and freed from that." She sipped her cappuccino with ostentatious propriety.

By this time, Margot was looking at us over her glasses with one eyebrow raised. "You know what I mean. We don't use *bad* as a noun."

Daryl started whistling a recognizable tune from Ennio Morricone. Jess paused for a moment, then named the movie Daryl had in mind: "*The Good, the Bad, and the Ugly*!" She high-fived him. He turned to Margot: "*The bad*."

"But you're not referring to your group of bad people!" Margot said.

"Well," I said, "why can't we have a bad if we can have a good? You know, a good as in a good thing done? Here – let me give an example." I turned to my laptop and opened a recently viewed article, Nicholas Kristof's "Most Valuable Helper." "Manute Bol," I said, summarizing, "a seven-and-a-half-foot NBA star player originally from Sudan who died just this past weekend – June 19, 2010 – was so focused on building multifaith schools to help bring peace in his native country that he not only got his fans to donate to the cause, he not only buttonholed members of congress for it, he donated most of his own wealth. The first school will open soon. Is that not a good? Has he not done a good?"

"Well, yes," Margot said, "but it's not really idiomatic to say that one has done a bad. It sounds like child talk, in fact."

"Perhaps it's from the talk of a non-native speaker," I offered.

"Well, I wonder if that's where it came from."

I was smiling as I tapped a few more keys and pulled up a Language Log post by Geoffrey Pullum, "Pick-up basketballism reaches Ivy League faculty vocabulary." "In fact, it has its origins in pick-up basketball games at the collegiate level. In the 1980s, it came to be popular to say *my bad* if you made a bad pass or missed an opportunity – similar to how a chorister might raise his or her hand after singing a wrong note in rehearsal, to acknowledge the fault. Now, that might indicate an origin in African-American Vernacular English. But actually, there's some pretty good evidence – as you'll see here –" I turned the laptop towards Margot – "the person who started it was not a native speaker of English. He was a native speaker of Dinka, a Nilo-Saharan language. It caught on probably in part because he was such a salient player. Here's a quote from a *USA Today* article written after he turned pro." I pointed at the screen.

Margot read it out: "After making a bad pass, instead of saying 'my fault,' Manute Bol says, 'my bad.' Now all the other Warriors say it too."

Daryl had an impressed and pleased look. Jess, grinning widely, said, "Well, I think his good was good enough that we can take his bad!"

illeist

MARCUS BRATTLE, MY (DE)MENTEE, is at that impressionable, mercurial, protean age where nearly every meeting is a manifestation of some new bent. The latest is hip-hop and dancehall, which sits a bit oddly on his British-accented tongue. At our most recent meeting, as he slouched up to the dining room table in his house wearing an exceedingly baggy T-shirt and idiotically baggy pair of pants, plus a backwards ball cap with – um, yes, I think it indeed is – fake cornrows dangling from it, I had cause to remind myself of the merits of how much his mother is paying me and how good her espresso is.

"Yo yo yo, de Mar-*cuss* is here." He flopped down and started rapping through a bit of "Eye Deh A Mi Knee" by Sean Paul: "We keep drilling it and we keep filling it and all this time say we never put a pill in it. The gal them say them love how we still in it, we free willin' it and we know we can't stop killin' it... Ever thrillin' it, we value and we illin' it and from we deh 'bout inna them life nothing ill in it..."

"De Mar-*cuss* has evidently been practising," I observed drily.

"De Mar-*cuss* is ill at it. Now he be illin' it. De Mar-*cuss* is licensed to ill."

Cute. A Beastie Boys reference. "De Mar-*cuss* is certainly a beastly boy," I said. "He is also become an illeist, I see."

"De Mar-*cuss* is *de* illest!"

"Not *illest*," I said. "*Illeist*. Rhymes with *silliest*. Resembles it too." I had a sip of espresso.

Marcus looked at me warily. "Yo, what dat, yo?"

"It's not *yo*, and it's not *you*. More to the point, it's not *I*, it's *he*. An illeist is someone who refers to himself – or herself, though guys seem more prone to it in my experience – in the third person. Like Bob Dole, who always said 'Bob Dole will do this' and 'Bob Dole believes that.'"

"Who's Bob Dole?"

Pause. Mental readjustment on my part. "A guy who ran for president of the US before you were born. Never mind. ...It comes from Latin *ille*, meaning 'he'. It's constructed in contrast with *egoist*, which is formed on *ego*, meaning 'I'. It's a bit ironic, because illeists tend to be egoists, I find."

"Yo, it sounds important. It sounds famous."

"It sounds like Bucky Katt from the comic strip *Get Fuzzy*."

"Ouch."

"I actually like that Latin word *ille*, though," I said. "The shape of it makes me think of my hair standing on end when I hear an illeist. And if you say it in the proper Latin way, it has a luscious double *l* – 'eel lay'."

"An eel lay? Oh, that's ill, man."

"Well, never mind, in English it's said like 'illy'." I knocked back the rest of my espresso.

Marcus smirked. "I have news for you," he said, back in his usual dialect. "I'm not the illeist. You are."

I cocked my head skeptically. "How so?"

"That espresso of which you're so fond. What brand did you think it is?" He gestured towards the kitchen, wherein I could see a can of Illy espresso. "That makes you the Illy-ist." He launched into a bit of the Beastie Boys: "But I'm chiller with the Miller – cold coolin' at the bar. I can drink a quart of Monkey and still stand still. What's the time? – it's time to get ill."

I stared at my empty cup. "It is indeed."

tmesis

MY WORD TASTING CLASS were having the discussion that all linguistics students have sooner or later, usually when covering morphology.

"So if I say *absofreakinglutely*, what is that?" Kayley asked.

"Rather tame!" Anna said. "I'd say –"

Kayley cut her off. "I know what you'd say. But what do we call it? It's like we're splitting *absolutely* into a prefix and a suffix and sticking them onto *freaking*."

"Only," said Brian, "it's really *absolutely* that's being modified and *freaking* that's doing the modifying. So it's an infix. And for any word you can predict where it will be infixed."

"Only it's not, really," I said. "What's a key feature of an affix? What kind of a morpheme is an affix? A prefix, a suffix: *pre, un, ness, ing*... Can I use them as independent words?"

"Nope," said Anna. "They're stuck freaking tight. Hangers-freak-ing-on."

Brian nodded. "They're bound morphemes."

"Bound and freaking gagged," Anna added.

"That would be nice," Kayley said purposefully at Anna.

"An an infix is also an affix," I said, "just one that's wedged in the middle." I tried to ignore Anna adjusting her shorts in response. "We don't have them in English. So the best word for this phenomenon, I would say, is *tmesis*." I wrote it on the board.

Jenna put up her hand. "I can't read your handwriting. It looks like you have a *TM* at the start of the word."

"That's what it is," I said. "From Greek for 'a cutting'." I said it again: "T'mee-zis."

Rupert raised his hand. "That sounds like the capital of Georgia."

Jenna looked incredulously at him. "It sounds like *Atlanta*?"

"The country of Georgia, in the caucasus," I said. "The capital of which is Tbilisi."

Brian was sitting back with his arm on the back of his chair, half-smiling. "It looks like a trademark infection."

"Abso-Fuddrucker's-lutely!" Anna giggled. "In-Viagra-fected!"

"Well, we might as well say 'trademarkesis'," Jenna declared. "We don't start a syllable with 'tm' in English."

"Except in this word," I said. "But I know what you mean. It trips and stumbles when you say it, more like something was taken out than put in. To look at it, it looks like the *m* was just wedged in there, doesn't it? Like the word is somehow *misset*, mixed up."

"So *tmesis* means putting a word inside another word," Brian said.

"Well, and there's the rub," I said. "Originally, classically, it meant inserting a word into a compound or set phrase. Like what Anna did with those phrases: *Hangers-freaking-on*. Or like saying *Superduperman* instead of *Superman*. Or even *whatsoever* instead of *whatever*, or *chit and chat* instead of *chit-chat*. Always fitting between the parts of a compound."

"So not *absofreakinglutely*?" Kayley asked.

"It breaks it right in the middle of a morpheme," I said. "Just like we would say *heli-freaking-copter* even though classically the split point would make it *helicofreakingpter*. So actually the word stuffed in is a rude interruption."

Rupert raised his hand.

"Yes?" I said.

"Which seems to be the point," he observed. "These words are rude, and they interrupt the main word. Rudely."

"But rhythmically," Anna said. I was so used to her making off-colour tangents that it took me a moment to realize this wasn't one. Or at least wasn't just one.

"Indeed," I said. "They stuff in right before a stressed syllable – primary or secondary stress. Now, that's not what most references will tell you tmesis involves. So… tmesis or not tmesis? That is the question."

"Absoscrewingbluingtattooinglutely," Anna declared.

Brian had a clever-looking smile. "We can even use it to prove that tmesis doesn't break English phonotactics. By proving that it has three syllables."

I paused for just a moment. "You're right, in fact." I turned to the class. "Where would you put the tmesis in *tmesis*?"

"That sounds like autocopulation," Anna said. "Tumescence!"

Kayley determined to oblige with a response to my question. "T'-freaking-alright-OK-shut-up-already-Anna-mesis!"

elope

DARYL AND I, PREPARING for the monthly Words, Wines, and Whatever tasting event at Domus Logogustationis, walked into the kitchen, where we happened on Maury, seated at the table, wearing one of his wonted looks of weary beleaguerment. He was eating a melon bitterly.

"Why so low, Joe?" Daryl said.

"My aunt eloped," Maury said.

"Oh dear," I said. "Your aunt eloped? To play?"

Maury gave me a look that suggested he was considering uttering some seldom-heard discouraging words.

"Wait," said Daryl. "Your aunt ran off to get married?"

"Well, yes, she did," Maury said, "when she was much younger. It was a bit of a family scandal, but only a bit. It saved my grandparents a lot of money, and everyone saw it coming. So when she threw her suitcase out the bedroom window, went downstairs and announced she was going to go buy some milk, her father simply said, 'Get some flowers while you're at it,' and gave her a dollar. My mother said, 'Good luck,' and off she went to the waiting car."

Daryl was momentarily nonplussed. "…And this accounts for your current funk?"

"Well, no," Maury said. "That was just the first in what has shaped up to be a habit."

"You can elope more than once?"

"I say," I said. "I think we must taste *elope* tonight. You didn't know that 'run away to get married' isn't the original meaning? That sense has only been around since the nineteenth century."

"Well, it means 'run away', anyway, right?" Daryl said. "The *lope* is the same one as in *lope* meaning 'leap' and is cognate with German *laufen*, 'run'."

"The oldest sense in English," Maury said, "was 'run away from one's husband with one's lover'. You can tell that that one comes from the fourteenth century – that was the ideal of romantic love back then: romance didn't lead to marriage, it led away from it."

"So your aunt ran away from her husband?" Daryl said.

"More than once," Maury replied. "As I said, it came to be a habit. And then she'd elope from the lover she'd eloped to. Sometimes she eloped to another lover and sometimes back to her husband. He was a patient man. And not an altogether faithful one."

"So who'd she elope from this time?"

"The nursing home."

"You can't elope from a nursing home!" Daryl exclaimed.

"In fact, she *took* a cantaloupe when she eloped this time. But, yes, you *can* elope. It's the term nursing homes use when one of their inmates goes AWOL."

I chuckled. "It certainly always gives me an image of seniors running away to get married."

"I wouldn't put it past her," Maury said. "They've found her in some interesting places on previous elopements."

"Well," said Daryl, "what's knocked you for a loop this time?"

Maury took a bite of his melon and considered his response.

"Hey," I said, "where'd you get the cantaloupe, anyway? It's not on the menu."

Just then a winsome septuagenarian in a nightdress came out of the pantry. "Lovely place you have here," she said. "Where do you keep the words?"

"Gentlemen," Maury said to us, "meet my aunt Susan."

Susan

Maury's aunt Susan, lately eloped from her nursing home, pulled up a chair in the kitchen of Domus Logogustationis. "I'm pleased to meet you gentlemen," she said, smiling prettily. "I'm Susan. I can't remember my current surname at the moment, but it doesn't really matter. It's not my first, and it may not be my last."

"Pleased to meet you," Daryl and I both said. Maury said nothing, having known her all his forty-two years.

"I thought I'd have a night out from the residence," she said. Plucking at her nightdress, she added, "I'm more dressed for a night in, but I learned a long time ago that if you look like you're going to leave, people may try to stop you. Anyway, I heard you taste words here, and that sounded like a kind of diet I could go on. I regret not having one to bring to the table. Certainly my name isn't much for the palate."

"*Susan?*" I said. "Plenty to go on there. Almost too much, in fact."

"*Brown-eyed Susan, black-eyed Susan,*" Daryl said. "Both flowers, though ironically *Susan* – or rather *Susanna*, which it comes from – means 'lotus flower'."

Susan smiled even more and folded her legs up on her chair. "Lotus I can do! I used to be a flower child. A late bloomer, though – I was thirty-three in the summer of sixty-nine. I was like the Suzanne who takes you down to her place near the river… Only, of course, I was Susan."

"So," Maury said, "you'd take them down to see what en*sues an'* all that." His vaguely weary, knowing manner telegraphed that Maury had heard many tales of her colourful life.

A thought occurred to Susan. "Wait, doesn't *Susanna* mean 'lily'? Which is twice as ironic!"

"Yes," said Maury, who it seemed had told her this before, "'lily' – or also 'rose'."

"Not the rose of Sharon!" Susan giggled.

"The source seems ultimately to be from Egyptian for 'lotus', though," Maury continued, "as Daryl says. But the Hebrew root for *Shoshana*, which is 'rose' or 'lily', is also from a verb meaning 'be joyous'."

"Well, that suits me!" Susan said. "Oh, Susanna, don't you cry for me... I've come from Alabama with a banjo on my knee. Or anyway from East York with a Band-Aid on my elbow." She pulled up her sleeve. Nope. She pulled up the other. Nope. "Hmmm... Either that was another time or it's on another body part..."

Maury leapt in to distract her from the search. "You never went by *Sue*, though."

"Nope!" she said, looking up. "I didn't want to have a name that was a constant reminder of legal action. Not that I'm all that keen on imputations of laziness."

"Nobody who knows you would ever call you lazy, Susan," Maury said. He left it unsaid that legal complications might be more common, given her storied adventuresomeness.

"I did try *Susie* on for size," she said, "in fifty-six or fifty-seven... Of course I'm not a Susie Q. But 'Wake Up, Little Susie' was my theme song... Well, it came second after 'Sleep with Me, Little Susie,' which was very popular." She giggled mischievously; Maury looked a bit uncomfortable.

"*Susan* is a popular name," I offered. "Several of my junior high school teachers were named *Susan*. Well, they were named *Mrs. This* and *Mrs. That*, but we found out they had first names, and they always seemed to be *Susan*."

Susan raised her hand. "I was a teacher for a time. But I prefer to be thought of as like Susan Sarandon. Or maybe Susan Sontag. Anyway," she added, stretching and shaking out her long hair, "I always liked the shape of the word, with those two sinuous *s*'s, even if I never liked the buzzing sound in the middle."

Daryl and I looked at Maury. "How come she hasn't been a member of the Order of Logogustation for years?" I asked him.

Maury paused and looked a bit uncomfortable as he tried to find a nice way to put it. Susan just laughed. "I'm not very reliable, and neither is my brain. I have episodes. I forget things. Now, of course, many people my age spend time thinking about the hereafter – they come into a room and say, 'Now, what was I here after?' – but while I've been a bit of a menace to society since at least nineteen fifty-four, I've been a bit much of a menace to myself from time to time since... what year is it now?"

"Two thousand ten," Maury said.

"Good grief," Susan said. "I'm seventy-five. Wait – what month is this?"

"August," Maury said.

"I'll be seventy-five soon. You must come to my birthday party."

The word "party" reminded Daryl. "We have a party to set up for." He turned to Susan. "You will stay?"

"That's why I'm here! I'm not just sussin' the place out..." She turned and looked at Maury and the melon that was before him. "I brought a cantaloupe. You can use what's left of it if you want." She swatted Maury lightly on the shoulder. "Piggy." She turned back to me and Daryl. "Now, I think I heard something about wine?"

tittup

I WAS SERVING AS VIRGIL to Maury's aunt Susan as she paid our monthly Words, Wines, and Whatever tasting a visit. It was clear that she was enjoying all three of the titular enticements. "Dear," she said, taking a refill of her wine, "I have an ounce, next I have two, and then it's three, and I'm off! I believe that's what my doctors call *titration*."

"I must say your graduated dosing is a good example of *titrimetry*," I said.

"To trim a tree?" she echoed. "It's not Christmas, but we certainly are opening some nice gifts of words here. I find it quite titillating."

A voice from behind said "*Titillating?*" Oh dear. It was Ross Ewage. He stepped forward. "Down to the last jot and tittle?"

"Oh, hello," said Susan, turning.

"Ross, this is Maury's aunt Susan," I said. "Susan, this is Ross Ewage."

"Raw sewage?" Susan said.

"I'm a veritable effluvium," Ross said. "Don't worry," he added, shaking her hand, "hands clean, mouth dirty." He pulled some small note cards out of his pocket, a word on each. "I overheard you sampling some words on my current theme: *titration, titillating*... Perhaps you would like to try some more."

"What's your theme?" Susan asked.

"I call it 'Show Me Your –'" He broke off as I suddenly aspirated some wine and started coughing. "You alright?" he said.

"Um, fine," I croaked, and swallowed some more wine to make the first bunch go down more smoothly.

"The wine is getting to us, I think," Susan said.

"Soon you'll be titubating," Ross said, holding out a card with that word written on it.

"That sounds naughty," Susan said with a little smirk.

"The implications are staggering," Ross said. Susan turned over the card and saw that *titubate* means "stagger, reel, stumble" and comes from Latin.

"Well, I must apologize for my appearance," Susan said, indicating her nightdress. "I could use a touch of titivation." (Which means "sprucing up" and is fake Latinate, formed probably on the basis of *tidy*.)

"Well, no one's asking you to tittup," Ross said. Susan raised one eyebrow slightly; Ross handed her another card.

"Three *t*'s," Susan said. "Not a triple *x*. I trust that *tup* here doesn't mean what *tup* means by itself." She flipped the card. "'Prance like a horse'. Onomatopoeic. Oh, and there's a noun, too. Which can also mean 'impudent hussy' or 'minx'." She handed Ross his cards back. "How could I possibly have made it to seventy-five without ever being called a *tittup*? Alas, I guess it's just not a common word, even if its object is common." She smiled sweetly. "What other words have you there? Perhaps *titmouse*?"

"Naturally," Ross said. "A nice name for a little bird, and a good example of reanalysis, as it has nothing to do with either of its ostensible roots."

"Oh, yes, I know about birds," Susan said. "I used to be quite the avid birdwatcher."

"I like watching birds," Ross said.

"I bet you do," Susan said with a little smile. "One I particularly like can't be found here in North America, though. The *Parus major*. It can have up to forty different calls and songs. Oh, now, *Parus major*..." She looked thoughtfully upward. "What do they call those in English?"

"*Great tits*," Ross said.

"Why, thank you," Susan tittered, smoothing her nightdress. She patted Ross on the cheek and teetered off towards the bar.

carboy, demijohn, delope

THE WORDS, WINES, AND WHATEVER tasting event was drawing to a close, and Maury's aunt Susan, eloped from her nursing home, was feeling delightful. "Maury!" she said, throwing her arm around her nephew. "My glass is empty. The bottle is empty. Fetch me a carboy." She tittered as she titubated.

"Fetch you a car?" Maury said. "Shall I call you a cab?"

"No, you silly thing, call me your aunt. I didn't say I wanted a car, boy. I've had more than enough cars and boys and boys in cars in my life. I said I wanted a carboy." She giggled again. "A large glass jug."

Maury sighed. "I feel you need to be contained."

"I'd take a demijohn. Though a demijohn often leads to a full john." She smiled happily and, looking around, spotted a still-unopened bottle of champagne by the bookshelf. "Maury, my boy. I want to look something up. Let's repair to the bookcase."

"What would you like to look up?"

"A Scotsman's kilt!" She giggled some more. "I want to explore the origins of *carboy* and *demijohn*."

They made their way to the shelf; Susan positioned herself in such a way that the bottle was not obvious to Maury but was within her reach. She pulled out an etymological dictionary. "Funny two words for glass jugs both sound like names for patrons of prostitutes." She flipped some pages. "Of course, I'm sure those demi-Johns and car boys like nice jugs." She found her page: "From Persian *qaraba*, 'large flagon'. Ay qaraba! A loaf of bread, a jug of wine, and thou."

"A flagon," Maury said. "I think you're flaggin'."

She flipped some more pages. "Now… Is *demijohn* from Persian too? Or Arabic? Oh, I see: cognates in Persian and Arabic seem to have been borrowed from the French, as our word is: from *Dame Jeanne*, 'Lady Joan', because it looks like a fat lady. This word has had a change of sex!"

"Not one, but two, cases of reanalysis," I said. "Under the influence of alcohol, quite evidently."

"Speaking of which…" Susan grabbed the champagne bottle and started to undo the foil.

"The evening is concluding," Maury protested. "You really must return."

"I eloped at the beginning of the evening," Susan said, "and once I have dealt with this small matter I will delope."

"*Delope* isn't related to *elope*, though," Maury said. "It's a pistol dueling term; it means 'fire into the air'."

"I know," said Susan. "I've read books by Georgette Heyer. One does it when one's opponent is simply not up to one's level. And, Maurice, lad, you are not as looped as I. Therefore, I must delope." Whereupon she popped the champagne cork into the air. It whizzed past Maury's ear and ricocheted off the ceiling.

Maury took the bottle from her, drank a good draught straight from it, and handed it back. "Time for the genie to go back in the bottle," he said, and went off to arrange for a taxi.

whimsy

JESS HAD JUST COME INTO THE KITCHEN at Domus Logogustationis, where Daryl, Margot, and I were lolling about. "It looks like something's moving in your jacket," Daryl said, eyeing Jess's windbreaker. He looked again, blinked. "Wow, that was weird. Gave me the whim-whams."

"More likely the fantods, you mean," Margot remarked. "A whim-wham is more like a fantastic notion."

"Or a fantastical object," I said. "Or an ornament of dress. Like, say, a little pair of cat ears on a brooch." I gestured to Jess's neckline, where just such an ornament was apparent.

Then the ornament turned its head and mewed.

"Gentlemen," Jess said, "and lady, meet Whimsy."

We reacted as you might expect, kittens being the cutest things in all of creation: "Awww!" We clustered around.

"What gave you the notion to name it *Whimsy*?" Daryl asked. Jess responded with a don't-feed-me-straight-lines raised-eyebrow look.

"Is this a *he* or a *she*?" Margot asked.

"A *him*," Jess said. "There is, after all, a *him* in *Whimsy*."

"What made you decide to get a kitten?" I asked.

Jess gave me the same kind of look she had given Daryl. But then she decided to answer anyway. "Well, it wasn't whimsy or some whim. It's always unwise to get a pet on a notion – they're a commitment. No, I had decided that I needed a touch of whimsy in my life. And here – ow!" The kitten was climbing up her shirt and onto her shoulder.

"Was that a whimper?" I asked.

"Not that I'm a wimp or anything," she said. She stroked Whimsy. "Well, listen up and you'll hear a Whimsy purr." Pause. "Speaking of purr, I came in here to find some milk. And a saucer. Now where, how, what…" She looked around.

"Don't forget *whom*, *when*, and *why*," Margot observed dryly.

"Ah, well," Jess said, striding towards the cupboards, "my favourite *wh* word is definitely *whimsy*. Once you've done with the details you still need flights of fancy."

"As long as your whims don't carry you with the winds," Margot said.

"Why don't *you* have a cat?" Daryl asked Margot.

"If I did, I'd more likely have quinsy. Tonsillitis. I'm allergic."

"So am I," I sighed. "One of the great tragedies of my life." Margot opened her mouth to issue another correction; I pre-empted it. "Yes, I know that it's not technically a tragedy: there is no *hubris*, no *hamartia*, no *climax*, no *crisis*... let it go."

"Speaking of 'let it go,'" Jess said, attempting to lift the kitten off her shoulder, "Whimsy has developed a whimsical attachment to my shirt." She shrugged off her jacket and tried again to get the kitten delicately off her shirt, which appeared to be made of silk. "Oww."

Daryl lent a hand and lifted the kitten off. Unfortunately, the result was a noticeable tear in the shirt.

"Huh," Jess said, poking her finger into the hole. "Flimsy."

skiving

"ALRIGHT," I SAID TO young Marcus Brattle, "let's get down to work, and no skiving."

We were at the dining room table at his house, my young mentee and I, and today's topic was syntax. Marcus had not so far warmed very much to the syntax trees I was having him draw.

"Skiving," Marcus said. "Sounds like good sport."

"And you're always game for good sport," I said. "But let's start by drawing a tree for that sentence: 'Skiving sounds like good sport.'"

"No, but what I mean is, it sounds rather like *skydiving*."

"Indeed it does," I conceded. "With a little insertion. And looks like *skindiving*, with a little insertion."

"In fact," said Marcus, writing the word out, "it looks like *skiing*, with just a little *v* in the middle carving a snowplow through it. You know, I'd like to ski for a living. But of course if you do it for a living it's not skiving. Sport is much more fun when you're getting away from work to do it."

"Getting away – but are you simply carving off, perhaps darting quickly and lightly as another meaning for *skiving* has it, or slinking away, as French *esquiver* – a possible source for *skive* – means?"

"Slinking away in something slinky?" Marcus said. "Perhaps your skivvies?"

"I would think that would be a short break."

"But you know," Marcus said, "this word conceals a horde of *Vikings*."

"And is raiding other towns and countries a way to shirk work, the ultimate laddish road trip," I asked, "or is it work itself? I'm inclined to think the latter, since *skiving* is often used in the army to refer to dodging duty."

"Dodging mopping and boring things like that," Marcus said. "Everyone likes marauding and destroying. It's fun."

It occurred to me that Marcus had, in his little way, some direct knowledge of the enjoyability of marauding and destroying.

"Well," I said, "but the point is that with skiving there's no *risking*." I wrote the rearranged letters and showed the *v* pinching together to become an *r*.

"There's risking getting pinched," Marcus said, meaning getting caught. "There's risking your mentor noticing that you're not doing any work."

I paused and raised an eyebrow. He had succeeded in diverting the work he didn't like for a couple of minutes already.

"But thanks," Marcus added with a little smile, "for being a good sport."

stench, stanch, staunch

"Oyyy," I said, stepping into Domus Logogustationis, local headquarters of the Order of Logogustation. "What's the stench?"

"There's been a little backup," Maury said, gesturing towards the lavatory. "We've had to call for backup."

A tall, angular fellow in overalls came out of the washroom. Seeing me, he took off a glove and came over, extending a hand in greeting. "Hi. I am Stan."

"Stan," I said, shaking hands with him. "From *Stanley*, taken from Old English for 'stone meadow'."

"No, in fact," Stan said. "Taken from *Zdenek*. I am from the Czech Republic originally."

"*Zdenek*," Maury said. "From Latin *Sidonius*, 'person from Sidonia.'"

"Yes," Stan said. "I anglicized. I began to tire of people mispronouncing my name. All these people who think they can't say 'zd'. Even though English is full of 'st'."

"Well, Zdenek," I said, "are you able to stanch the stench?"

He patted me on the shoulder amicably. "I am your staunch ally. But stanching is not the solution, it is the problem. The pipe is blocked."

"And the solutions in it are not draining," Maury quipped. "They are stagnant."

"In fact. But this is not something I can fix with a snake. I will need to bypass it with another pipe."

"A stent," I said before I could stop myself.

"That's the extent of it," Stan said. "I will affix it to a stanchion for support."

"That's quite the stunt," I said.

"Well," Stan said, smiling indulgently, "it is just because the pipe has been stunted. But let me finish the work now so that my stint here does not go too long." He turned and went back to the washroom.

"Interesting," Maury said, "the different effect of affricate versus stop at the ends of these words. *Stench* and *stink* come from the same Old English word, but *stink* seems more acute and *stench* perhaps more thoroughgoing."

"I'm sure *drench* and *quench* and such words have some effect on *stench*," I said. "Plus the wetness of the fricative portion at the end."

"The vowels, too," Maury noted. "The vowel movement between *stench* and *stink* is rather like that between *stauunch* and *stanch*, which are even more closely related, being actually different forms of the same word: verb 'stop the flow of water', adjective 'impervious to the flow of water', both from Old French and possibly ultimately related to the Latin etymon of *stagnant*."

"The velar /k/ stop is stickier and, I would say, denser in feeling than the lighter alveolar /t/ stop," I said. "*Stint* – 'cease action' or 'a limited period of action'; *stunt* – 'stop the development of' or 'athletic display'; *stent* – 'temporary medical bypass or drainage tube'. None of them as strong in the sound as *stink, stank, stunk*."

"Two from Old English and one eponym," Maury said, reflecting on *stint, stunt,* and *stent.* "I'm not sure where the family name of the good dentist Dr. Charles Stent came from."

An encouraging sound of gurgling came from the washroom. Maury and I went over to look. Stan appeared to have solved the problem. "That was quick," I said.

"Well, gentlemen," Stan said, arising, "when you are well trained, the draining takes over. So I have given you express service. But I hope," he added, taking off his gloves and reaching for his invoice pad, "when you write a cheque to Stan the Czech you will be unstinting."

pants

I WAS BACK TUTORING young Marcus Brattle again after the Christmas break, planted in the dining room in his house. As usual, he was trying to distract from studying. His sally this time was "Get anything nice for Christmas?"

"Some nice pants," I said, and stood up to show him.

He recoiled. "Spare me!"

Ah, yes. Young Marcus and his family moved to Canada from England only a couple of years ago. "I mean what you'd call *trousers*," I said. "Not what we'd call *underpants*."

Marcus let out a little noise of relief. "Funny word, *pants*," he said.

I sat back down. "Because you use it to refer to an undergarment when in fact it was originally an outer garment, pantaloons, named after a character from Commedia dell'Arte who wore them?"

"No," he said. "Like I'd know that."

"You do now," I said. "It is funny, though, as many people have remarked, that not only *pants* but *trousers, slacks, shorts, skivvies, gotchies*, et cetera, including derivative words such as *shorts, undies, panties, and briefs*, are all plural, while *shirt, jacket*, and so on are singular."

"I would have thought you'd know why that is," Marcus said.

"I *do* know," I said. "The two legs used to be made and donned as separate parts, just like stockings and hose."

"*Hose* is singular," Marcus observed.

"Go figure," I said. "Actually, oddly, it's a mass object." ("I object to some odd masses I see in pantyhose," Marcus offered while I continued talking.) "Anyway," I said, "the plural has by long tradition become attached to anything worn below the waist that has separate legs or at least separate leg holes. Even new products will tend to take that on."

"Not a thong," Marcus pointed out.

"Well, *thong* is actually originally a strap, so in the case of the undergarment it's referring to the butt floss, which is one thing." ("Classy,"

Marcus interjected at "butt floss.") "When I was a kid, I used to wear thongs to the beach —"

"Naw! Augh!" Marcus waved his hands as if battling cluster flies. "Stop!"

"— by which we meant sandals with strapping that connected to the sole between the first two toes. The strapping being the thong and, in that case too, transferring the name to the whole object."

"Well," said Marcus, "there's many a man who *pants* at the sight of a thong. On the right person!"

"The verb *pant* does happen to be cognate with the noun *fantasy*," I noted drily.

"Funny word, *pants*," Marcus said (again).

"Because of the plurality and all that."

"No, because in England it's an insult. 'That's just pants, that is!'"

"But you wouldn't say 'That's just knickers' or 'That's just trousers,'" I said.

"No," Marcus said. "Except for *your* trousers, maybe."

I stood up to display them. "You don't like them?"

"They're pants," he said.

"Obviously," I said. "Welcome to Canada."

je ne sais quoi

WE HAD A COUPLE OF GUESTS at our monthly Words, Wines, and Whatever tasting event: Jenna, lately graduated from Tufts University, and passing through town at just the right time; and Maury's aunt Susan, who this time had come escorted by Maury rather than having eloped from her nursing home.

"I find the word *exquisite* exquisite," Jenna said. "It has a certain... what would be the right way of putting it?"

"*Je ne sais quoi*," said Susan.

"Yes! Exquisite has a certain *je ne sais quoi*," declared Jenna. "Thank you."

"Actually," Susan said, smiling politely, "I meant to say that I didn't know what the right way of putting it would be. Words sometimes... well, they don't fail me so much as pass me – without stopping. I'm more well aged than a fine wine. *Jeunesse, c'est quoi?*"*

"You sound quite erudite to me," Jenna said. "It's interesting, though: I'm used to *je ne sais quoi* having only three syllables." (She pronounced it like "jun say kwa.")

"Well, then, *jeune, c'est quoi?*" said Susan. "It does seem like a typically French phrase, with that amorous touch – the little moue you make when saying *je*, the air kiss you make with the *quoi* – ah, kissing air. I suppose if I were to stick to that my life would have less trouble. And less fun. Or maybe not. *Je ne sais pas.* Well, when it comes to staying out of trouble, *je n'essaie pas.*" She smiled sweetly at Jenna, who returned that sort of glazed smile that says "I don't understand the language you're speaking but I'll pretend."

"It's interesting how in order to express the foreignness of something to us we retreat to a foreign phrase," Jenna said. "But I guess it's really a way of finessing the matter, by drawing on the perceived elegance of French. There's even a certain insouciance to it –" She lifted her wine glass with her left hand and made a gesture as though taking a drag on a cigarette and then waving it with her right hand: "Ah, je ne sais quoi!"

"Indeed," said Susan. Jenna's gesture reminded her of her glass of wine. "I do think that my *verre de vin* needs to be *rempli*. ...Now, doesn't that sound so much more cultured than 'My glass of wine needs to be refilled'?" She held out her glass to Maury.

"Well, we use many French-derived terms for the more refined things," Maury said – "*beef* and *pork* from the French for the meat, and *cow* and *pig* from English for the animals, for instance."

Susan kept holding out her glass. "Well, I do hope you're not saying this old cow is being a pig in wanting another glass, Maurice. Because if I don't get another drink, I don't know what-all."

"Not at all," Maury said, taking the glass. "Shall I bring some more canapés?"

"Oh, yes, one should not drink on an empty stomach. *À jeun, c'est quoi?*" She turned to Jenna. "*Voulez-vous aussi un autre verre de vin?*"

"Um..." Jenna hesitated, unsure what she was being asked.

Susan raised an eyebrow. "Jenna say, *'Quoi?'*" She picked up Jenna's glass and handed it to Maury. "Garçon! I think she needs a little more French in her."

    *French phrases used herein:

Je ne sais quoi: "I don't know what"

Jeunesse, c'est quoi?: "Youth, what's that?"

Jeune, c'est quoi?: "Young, what's that?"

Je ne sais pas: "I don't know"

Je n'essaie pas: "I don't try"

À jeun, c'est quoi?: "On an empty stomach, what's that?"

Voulez-vous aussi un autre verre de vin?: "Would you also like another glass of wine?"

Quoi?: "What?"

shirr

MAURY HAD INVITED A few of us – me, Elisa, and Jess – over for brunch, and was setting before us small dishes with eggs and butter floating in them.

"Mmm! What's this?" exclaimed Elisa Lively.

"It's a shirred egg," said Maury.

"Assured of what?" Elisa asked.

"Proper cooking and no absence of cholesterol," Maury said.

"But can you tell me what you did to it?"

"Shirr."

Pause.

"So what did you do to it?"

"Shirr." Maury was trying to suppress a smile. He has a wicked streak.

"Sure?"

"Yes, I'm sure."

"What are you sure about?"

"The eggs. I assure you, that egg is a shirred egg."

I gestured at the yellow goodness my egg was swimming in. "Butter you shirr?"

"Always."

"OK," said Jess, "stop milking this or I'll cream you."

Maury held up a finger, turned on his heel and went to his cookbook shelf. He returned with a copy of the 1977 English printing of the 1960 edition of the *Larousse Gastronomique*, open to page 338. He handed it to Elisa with a gesture. She read aloud: "'Eggs sur le plat, or shirred eggs.' ...Oh! ...You're funny. '...For two eggs coat the dish with one half tablespoon butter. Heat on the stove. Break the eggs into the dish and pour melted butter on the yolks. Cook in the oven for as long as is liked and when ready, sprinkle with fine salt.'" She handed the book back. "So I gather that to make shirred eggs, you shirr them."

"You gather correctly," Maury said. "In fact, if I may say 'sew,' when you shirr you always gather."

"OK, you've lost me again," Elisa said.

"The meaning of *shirr* is elastic," I explained.

"You guys!" Jess said. She turned to Elisa. "*Shirr* also means 'gather or draw up fabric using parallel threads', and a shirred garment has elastic threads woven into it. The noun *shirr* can mean elastic webbing."

"Oh," said Elisa. "What's the connection?"

"The elastic, of course," Maury said. Elisa swatted him. "Actually," Maury said, "I don't know, and the usual reference sources are not forthcoming on the subject. It may have to do with the appearance of the eggs when they are shirred."

"Well," said Elisa, determined to get a wordplay into the match, "I guess you're the shirriff today."

"No, this is the Shirriff," said Maury, gesturing to a jar of Shirriff marmalade that was on the sideboard. "And your toast." He pointed to a plate of toast on the table.

"I'm toast?" Elisa said.

"Don't egg him on," Jess said. "Look, I'm eating." She took a bite. "Why don't we all?"

"I hope it's good," Maury said.

Jess smiled a little. "Shirr." (Or perhaps she said "it is" in Mandarin. It sounds about the same...)

124

begroan

"THEY USED A HYPHEN in *wake up*, the verb!" Margot exclaimed. "How do they propose to spell *wake him up*, then? As *wake* hyphen *him* hyphen *up*?"

Daryl rolled his eyes and looked around the coffee shop to see if other eyes were turning yet. "Happy Friday afternoon," he said, raising his latte in mock toast.

"Come on," Margot protested. "These things matter."

"You are more apt than most people to begroan other people's usage," Daryl said.

Margot's eyes popped wide. "It would be very apt to *bemoan* your use of a non-word!"

"*Moan, groan*… how do you know *begroan*'s not a word?" Daryl said. He had pulled out his iPad and was tapping away at it.

"You meant *bemoan*," Margot said.

"If I'd meant *bemoan* I would have said *bemoan*," Daryl said with a flicker of a fake smile.

"Come, now," I said, "can't we *be groan*-ups? He used it, you understood it, it's a word."

"A word you won't find in any dictionary," Margot said.

"That may be," Daryl muttered, continuing to manipulate his iPad, "or that may not be. …A-*ha!*" He turned his iPad to Margot. It displayed the *be-, prefix* entry from the *Oxford English Dictionary*, scrolled to show "begroan v. to groan at" with a citation from 1837. Margot was nonplussed, or should I say bemused. "Pity there's no entry for *be-hatch*," Daryl said, "'cause I done be-hatched this on you, be-hatch!" He made the sort of hip-hop-style hand gesture that cretins from "reality TV" shows are fond of.

I took the iPad from him and started scrolling through the very long entry. "Boy, someone's been busy as a bee with all the *be*'s."

"But it doesn't even make sense," Margot protested, gesturing to the list. "I mean, a lot of these words have nothing to do with being something. When you think of *become*, that's 'come to be', right? And *bemoaning* is to be moaning, and *bejewelled* is to be with jewels, and so on."

"I think you'll have to leave that one *by*," I said. "The prefix *be-* is not from the verb *be*, it's from the preposition *by*. So adding *be* can add the sense of 'about', 'around', or 'throughout'; from that it took on a broader use as an intensifier, and also came to signify result – as in *bedimmed* – or object bestowed – as in *bewigged* – or an instrumental relation, as in *bewitch*." I started idly humming the tune from the TV show *Bewitched* as I continued to scroll.

"Oh, would you bequiet… yourself?" Margot grumbled.

"Perhaps you could becalm… yourself," I replied with a little smirk, and launched into another musical snippet: "Let it be, let it be…"

"Behave," Margot said.

"I'm being as have as I can," I said, giggling. Margot leaned over to look at what was in my cup.

"Perhaps," said Daryl, "you could bestow my iPad upon me, so I can be stowing it in my bag."

"Here you be," I said, handing it over. I turned to Margot, lifting my cup. "I only wish I were beliquored."

"You can't be telling me that's a word," Margot said.

Daryl lifted an index finger and scrolled quickly on the page. "Ah… yep. 'Beliquor, verb, to soak with liquor, to alcoholize.'"

Margot slouched back in her chair and threw her hands up. "I'm beleaguered." She reached for her coffee and slugged the rest of it back.

boot

"OH, THIS DOES NOT BODE WELL."

Marilyn Frack gazed with consternation at her laptop. In this case, I mean she was looking at her computer. She had been doing a presentation on constellation names when her computer froze on Boötes. She tapped at it a few times and then looked up with a slight pleading in her gaze. Everyone knew what that meant: time for the resident computer geek.

Daryl sighed. He got up and walked up to the table. "Let me have a look at it."

Marilyn stepped aside. "Well, I guess sometimes these things happen… and one has to pull oneself up by one's boöte-straps." She did a Hollywood flex, displaying thigh-high boots below her black leather skirt, with black fishnets to boot.

"Are those cowboy boots, then?" said Philippe Entrecote from the back of the room, in reference to Boötes being the herdsman, from Greek for 'ox-driver'.

"Reverse cowgirl, maybe," Marilyn said, winking at Edgar Frick, her other half.

"Um," said Daryl, not so much because he had something to say as to divert that line of discourse. "Well, ironically, my usual best efforts are proving bootless. Fittingly, I will have to reboot."

"Overall more fitting than ironic, then," I piped up, "since her boots and *reboot* are related and *bootless* is not."

Daryl looked up from the computer. "*Reboot* and *boot up* coming from a reference to pulling oneself up by one's bootstraps, yes," he said. "Because a part of the operating software loads the rest up."

"But what do you mean *bootless* is not?" Marilyn said, sitting on the table edge and peeling off her boots in as provocative a style as she could muster. "It seems related to me."

"It might or might not be related to you," I said, "but *bootless* meaning 'unavailing' and *to boot* meaning 'in addition' come from a different root than the Latin root of *boot* meaning 'footwear'. They have an old Germanic root meaning 'good' or 'advantage'. We mostly don't use it as such, but we use a related comparative form all the time."

"*Booter?*" Marilyn said.

"Perhaps *butter*," Edgar leered.

"Well," said Philippe from the back, "it *may* be related. He's referring to the conjectural *bat*, which may be related to *boot*; thanks to umlaut, *bat* in the comparative is *better*."

"Better than what?" Marilyn said, disingenuously, with a little smirk.

"A bat might be better used on your computer," Daryl said, forcing a second reboot.

Marilyn leaned over and batted her eyes at the machine. "Is that better?"

I turned to Philippe. "Did she just call herself a bat?"

"I believe she did," he said.

"Well," said Marilyn, turning to us, "here's boot and reboot." She flung a boot at me, and one at Philippe to boot. But her efforts were bootless – she missed, and we were not cowed.

spruce

THE OTHER DAY, I bumped into Maury in a clothing store in the mall. I almost didn't recognize him; he was wearing black pants and a black shirt and a leather vest.

"Good grief, man," I said, "have you been spending too much time with Frick and Frack?"

Maury swept his eyes over his own figure and said, "I know not what it shall signify…"

A tall, lean, stylish woman appeared from behind a clothing rack. "I am sprucing him up!" she declared, with what sounded like a German accent.

"James," Maury said, "this is Lorelei."

I shook her hand and tried, out of consideration for Maury, not to appear too obviously attracted to her. "How do you do."

"I may be Lorelei, but I am not from the Rhine," the goddess declared, smiling. "In fact, I was raised in East Berlin, and my mother was a child refugee from Königsberg. So I am Prussian."

"Hence the spruce jerkin," Maury explained, indicating his vest.

"You have said that already and I do not quite understand," Lorelei said.

"The word *spruce* actually comes from French *Prusse*, for 'Prussia,'" Maury said, "and a few different things imported from Prussia in medieval times came to be called *spruce*. Spruce fir, for one –"

"Oh, I do not wear fur," said Lorelei.

"No," said Maury, "F-I-R, the tree. *Fichte*. We call it *spruce*."

"Oh!" Lorelei looked informed. "This is what I have decorated my apartment with! Only it is from Norway. Do continue!"

"Anyway, fine leather from Prussia was *spruce leather*, and in particular a jerkin – a sleeveless jacket – made from it was a *spruce jerkin*. And spruce jerkins were considered very smart looking indeed. Around the time of Shakespeare, *spruce* came to be an adjective meaning 'stylish, trim, neat, dapper, smart.' From which we get the verb *spruce*, with or without *up*."

"So indeed I am sprucing you up!" Lorelei declared. "Only you are already smart. Now I am making you neat and stylish and dapper." She scanned his not-really-thin figure. "Trim will come." She smiled again. "Now, I have found you a tie. Come!" She gestured and began to walk away.

As Maury began to move away, I said, "Do you like your new look?"

He leaned close and said confidentially, "I feel like a jerk in it." Then he straightened up. "But it's all for a good cause."

"Or a good effect," I said, as he trotted off after Lorelei, who shouted back, "Oh, nice to meet you, James."

The next day, I saw him at the Domus Logogustationis. He looked a bit the worse for the wear. "I must say, you look a little blue," I said.

"In more ways than one," he replied. "We went to a gallery party and they were serving International Klein Blue cocktails, which are made with Prussian blue. It retains its colour as it passes through – you may be seeing a bit of it in my skin hue, perhaps."

"I don't think that accounts for your overall mien," I said. "I'm not sure any blue on you might not be a bruise."

"I think it is," he said, touching his upper back and wincing. "Well, after the party, she showed me her place."

"Was it good?" I asked. "Norwegian wood?"

"It was really spruce," he said. "She's quite the conversationalist. Did you know Königsberg is a link between Leonhard Euler and the Eagles?"

I paused for a moment. The lightbulb went on. "'Seven Bridges Road,'" I said.

"Not the only topological problem of the evening," he said. "We talked until two."

"She seems quite engaging," I said. "And then?"

"And then she said, 'It's time for bed.'" He sighed. "She told me she worked in the morning and started to laugh. I told her I didn't, and crawled off to sleep in the bath."

"Hence the bruise," I said.

"No," he said. "She turned out to be teasing me. She dragged me back and introduced me to her birch."

chai

WE HAD JUST SETTLED IN at the Metaphor Café ("Service with a Simile") – Daryl, Margot, Jess, and I – and were giving our orders to Jess, who had offered to go up and get our beverages.

"I'll have a chai tea latte," Daryl said.

Margot glanced at Daryl with a look of distaste. She put on a saccharin smile and turned to Jess. "I'll have a coffee café au lait with milk."

Jess arched her eyebrow just a little and paused for a moment. "… Regular with caffeine, or decaf without caffeine?"

"Why, regular with caffeine, of course."

I couldn't be bothered to play along. "Decaf latte, please, high-fat milk."

"Surely," Margot said, "you mean a decaf coffee caffè latte with milk without caffeine."

"Oh, for heaven's sake," Daryl said.

"You started it," said Margot.

Daryl threw up his hands. "OK, yes, I know, *chai* means 'tea'."

"Specifically spiced tea with milk," Margot said. "You might as well have asked for salsa sauce, or entered a PIN number into an ATM machine."

"The pleonasm police are out," Daryl said. "I shall be denied entry into high so-chai-tea."

"Actually," I said, as Jess sidled away to go place the orders, "*chai* is just Hindi for 'tea'. Tea with spices is *masala chai* in India. And that's normally made with milk, yes. So it's like *salsa*, which is just Spanish for 'sauce' – in English, the word is used with a more specific meaning that's further specified in the original language."

"But that's the way they've always had tea in India, isn't it?" Margot said. "From time immemorial?"

"Well, from before you were born, anyway," I said. "But tea was grown almost exclusively in China until the end of the 1800s, when the British began cultivating it on a large scale in India in order not to be dependent on China. And the Indians themselves didn't really drink it until the British-owned Indian Tea Association encouraged industries to provide tea breaks, in the early 1900s. That's when the chai wallahs with their tea carts started circulating. But the masala chai was a local invention that stretched out the tea leaves and added some spice. Literally and figuratively."

"*Chai* is very similar to the Mandarin word for 'tea'," Daryl said, "*cha*." (He said it properly, with a rising tone.) "Clearly cognate. So how did we get *tea*? The word, I mean." He held up a finger and pulled out his iPad to look it up.

"From Malay," I said.

"But tea cures your malaise," Daryl quipped as he typed and scrolled.

I got up and did a few fluid moves. "So does chai tea. I mean tai chi."

"Is that what that was," Margot said. "I thought it was the cha-cha-cha."

"Oh," said Daryl, showing his iPad screen, "/te/ is also from the Amoy dialect of Chinese. Probable source of the Malay word."

"Sure," I said. "And the phonological relation is clear. Stop and affricate, both voiceless, same location – tip of the tongue – and the vowels easily transformed one to another, /a/ to /aɪ/ and /e/ and, in English, /e/ to /i/ – just getting more and more steeped. Every language that I'm aware of that has a word for 'tea' bases the word on one of those three streams: *cha, chai, te*. But the relation isn't obvious to most non-linguists."

"It still doesn't excuse the redundancy," Margot said.

"Redundancy is often a good idea for clarity," I said. "I too find *chai tea* a little grating, but I understand why they do it – they need to specify that it's tea, for those who don't know, and at the same time the word *chai* has a specificity and that nice bit of the exotic that *spiced* wouldn't."

"And the *latte* for the milk," Daryl said.

Jess arrived with the beverages. "Wallah!" she said, setting down Daryl's chai.

"That's *voilà*," said Margot.

"No," said Daryl, "that's the chai wallah."

plank

As I was walking down the street, I encountered Marcus Brattle, my adolescent mentee. "Brilliant!" he exclaimed (that's British for "Great!"). He pulled out a camera. "You came along at just the right time."

I looked at him warily. "You have plans?" His plans typically translated into disasters or messes, often involving humiliation, sometimes mine.

"I'm the plan king!" He said. "In fact, I'm planking!"

Oh. The faddishness of youth. "Planking?" I said, disingenuously. "Is that short for *public wanking*?"

"Get over it," he said. He pointed to one of Toronto's newly installed racks of bike-share cycles, nearby on the sidewalk. "I'm going to extend myself like a plank across two of those bikes there, and you're going to photograph it so I can post it."

"Haven't people gotten board of that fad yet?"

"It's planks for the memories," Marcus said. "People have planked on some remarkable things and in some remarkable places."

"And fallen to some remarkable deaths," I said. "It's all just plankton for the whale of media fads."

"It's the exploratory spirit."

"Sort of like a negative of spelunking," I observed. "Going up and over instead of down and under. We get a spree of planking followed by spill and plunking. One might come to imagine that *plunk* is the past tense of *plank*."

"Where does that leave *plonk*, then?"

"*Plonk* is cheap wine," I said. "Possibly a play on *vin blanc*, though people do hear in it the sound of a cork being pulled or a bottle being, well, plonked on a table."

"Onomatopoeia followed by I'm-a-gotta-pee-a," Marcus said. It occurred to me that he had learned much from me, but probably not the right things. "And you can plink the glasses."

"I don't think anyone actually uses *plink* that way – for that it's *clink*, but tiddly-winks and musical instruments do plink."

"And where's *plenk*?"

"There is no *plenk*. It's *plink, plank, plonk, plunk*."

"All based on sounds," Marcus said. "After all, when you drop a plank on the floor, that's the sound it makes: *plank!*"

It does, I thought. However… "Actually, the word comes to us by way of various French versions – modern French has *planche* – originally from Latin, probably related to *plana*, flat."

"Well," Marcus declared, "I'm the planna here, and I plan to be flat. On… those two bikes right there." He indicated two bikes with about five feet of space between them. "You stand over there and take the photo when I'm ready." He pointed to the other side of the sidewalk.

I took the camera and walked to where there was a good angle. Marcus grabbed one bike with both hands and swung one leg up onto the other. Then the other leg. "Alright," Marcus grunted, "have you got it?"

"You're sagging," I said.

Just then a woman walked up and asked, "What's he doing?"

I turned to her. "Planking."

"Blanketing?"

"No, planking. Like salmon."

"Sounds fishy to me. Anyway, I want to use one of those bikes."

Just then I heard another grunt and turned to see Marcus collapsing onto the ground.

"Was that a plunk?" I said. The woman walked over to one of the bikes to take it away.

Marcus started dusting himself off and standing up. "Ow. Did you get a picture while I was holding it rigid?"

"Uh…" I looked at the camera. "Is *blank* close enough for you?"

Jennifer, juniper

MAURY'S UNCLE RED HAS a country place, and Maury wangled an invitation for a set of his friends to come up and spend the weekend. He intimated to me that he was bringing a new interest named Jennifer.

It was rather hot out when I arrived, so I quickly dropped my bags and changed into swim gear. I passed through the kitchen to grab a bevvy, but Maury said that he had some he was just fixing up that he would bring out shortly. So I made a beeline to the pool.

I was just setting down my towel when a fetching lady emerged through some ornamental heather near the pool's edge. "Hello," I said. "I'm James."

"Hi," she said. "I'm Gwen. In fact, I'm gwen into the pool."

I paused. "Oh, you must be Maury's friend. I thought your name was Jennifer. …Oh, wait."

"Yes, that's right," she said. "*Gwen* as in short for *Jennifer*."

"Because *Jennifer* is really a Cornish version of the name *Guinevere*," I said. "Yes, I've seen Shaw's *Doctor's Dilemma*."

"Yup," she said. She quoted from the play: "'My name is Jennifer.' 'A strange name.' 'Not in Cornwall. I am Cornish. It's only what you call Guinevere.' Well, thanks in part to Shaw, it's not so strange anymore. *Jennifer* is now about as plane as *Jane*, so I went with the English version and then shortened it to Welsh roots." This was true: *Guienevere* is from Welsh *gwen* 'white, fair, blessed, holy' and *hwyfar* 'smooth, soft'.

"You could have gone with *Gaynor*," I said. *Gaynor* is a variant of *Guinevere*.

"Ew. Didn't want to. 'I Will Survive' by Gloria Gaynor would be playing through my life. Anyway, it's getting common in England, and over here sounds a bit too much like *Gaylord*."

At this juncture Maury arrived with a pitcher of martinis and some glasses. "Ah," said Gwen, "you've brought my namesake."

"*Juniper* and *Jennifer* aren't really related," Maury said.

"Oh, *jenever* know," Gwen said, playing on Dutch for 'gin'. "Yes, yes, I know it's from Latin."

"And from *juniper*," I volunteered, "come *genever* and *genièvre* and ultimately *gin*."

"Maury mentioned that," Gwen said. "But I do like the similarity of sounds. *Jennifer* and *juniper* differ only in one vowel and one consonant, and those consonants are closely related."

"For all that," I said, "*Jennifer* has a bit more of a rustle as of heather, and *juniper* has a little more of a nip to it."

"Meanwhile, *Guinevere* starts with a *g* and all those variants on *juniper* begin with the letter *g*," Gwen said. "But Maury, dahling, can you give me mine with a twist? Since I'm by the pool."

Maury obliged and handed Gwen a decent-sized martini with a twist of lemon peel. She held it up in toast: "Gin gin!" Then she downed the whole glass and danced a quick little twist. But her foot caught on my towel and she spun into the pool with a bit of a flip and a bit more of a splash.

"Well," Maury observed as she resurfaced spluttering, "that was a double Gaynor."

"She did say she was Gwen in," I remarked.

"Ha," said she. "I will survive." She held up the martini glass that she was somehow still holding. "Arrr. Pirate Jenny wants a refill."

I looked at Maury as if to say, "You've found a winner." He just lifted an eyebrow and the jug and refilled her glass.

137

groundhog

MAURY AND I AND Maury's friend Gwen (Jennifer) were besporting ourselves at the pool at Maury's uncle Red's country place. More specifically, Gwen was swimming laps (in spite of being two martinis to the better), I was swimming a bit and standing a bit, and Maury was sitting in a deck chair, fully clad, on his third martini.

"You should come in!" Gwen shouted at Maury. "It's fun! Exercise does a body good!"

"I am of the conviction," Maury said, "that one's heart has only so many beats in a lifetime. Raising one's heart rate therefore shorten's one's life."

"I think I've pointed out the error in that reasoning before," I said. "For instance, because I exercise, my resting heart rate is about 20 beats per minute slower than it used to be when I didn't exercise. While I'm exercising, it averages about 80 beats per minute faster than my resting heart rate used to be, or 100 beats faster than my resting rate. But I only exercise six hours a week. So one twenty-eighth of my time is spent exercising each week. That means my average heart rate is... let's see, a difference of 100 averaged out over 28, just about three and a half... my average heart rate is about sixteen and a half beats per minute slower than it would be if I didn't exercise. Sixteen and a half times how many minutes are there in a lifetime?"

"Alright, I get the point," Maury said. "I nonetheless find this option more refreshing. And I'm less likely to drown."

"Except your sorrows."

"May they be few."

Just then, Maury's uncle Red strode out. "Lady and gentlemen, I would like to point out that the sky is darkening and there will soon be lightning."

I pulled myself up out of the pool. Gwen protested: "But that's why I'm in the pool! I'm lightening myself up!" Funny how the skinny ones always complain about their weight.

"You could end up blackened," Red said, "like catfish. C'mon in, food's a-fixing."

We retreated obligingly. I headed to my room to change. As I opened the door I heard a sudden scuffling noise, and I noticed the corner of the carpet turned up. But a first scan of the room showed no animate forms.

Hm.

I knelt down and looked lower. I found what I sought beneath the bedside table: a critter that looked like a gopher, but click-dragged to rather larger size. A groundhog. It was cowering and looking at me nervously.

I shouted into the hall. "Red! There's a groundhog in my room!"

Red came around the corner. "Oh fer... gracious mercy... He was in here yesterday. It's like *Groundhog Day*." Maury and Gwen appeared behind him.

"Well, we aren't all that far from Wiarton," I observed.

Gwen peeked down. "And he does look a bit like Bill Murray. I wonder what he's after in here."

"Some marmot-lade, perhaps?" Maury said. (Groundhogs are a kind of marmot.)

"Maybe it's looking for some wood to chuck," I said. (*Woodchuck* is another name for a groundhog.)

"Well," Red said, "he can chuck all the wood that a woodchuck chucks... outside. And hog the ground there too. Hand me that broom. And open that door." He gestured to the door to the outside that my room – actually a converted covered porch – featured. I went over and opened it. Maury handed Red the broom, and then grabbed a golf putter that was leaning against the wall.

Red looked at Maury. "What are you doing with that? We're trying to chase the poor thing out, not beat it to putty. I have all the ground hog I need in the kitchen. Oh, no vegans here, right? Because I'm making something I saw on Epic Meal Time."

"I'm just trying to help encourage it to go to ground," Maury said.

139

"Well, let's line up and make a path to the door for it. Coooome on, little guy... get the hell outa here." A little encouragement and some sweeping under the bed eventually resulted in our little friend making a break for it through the open door, which we swiftly closed.

"I wonder where it will go," Gwen said.

"Oh, it has plenty of room out there," Red said. "This used to be a farm. I've sold off most of the turf, but I still hogged enough of the ground for myself. Just as long as it stays away from my car."

"Have you seen Red's car?" Maury said. "It's in the barn. It's a brilliant red Barchetta."

"Bugatti," Red corrected him. "It's a real rush to drive."

"You don't need to worry about him stealing your car," Gwen said. "He's not Mr. Toad."

I, meanwhile, was standing there sounding out the various names of the beastie. "*Grrroundhoooggg...* round and rumbling... *Wood! chuck!* short and sharp... *Marrrmota monax...* murmuring up to a crack, like lightning in reverse..."

The heavens obliged at that moment with a crack of a lightning bolt not so far away and the following rolling rumble.

"Poor thing," Gwen said, looking out towards the groundhog's path of retreat. "What if the lightning zaps him?"

"It's OK," Maury said. "He's a natural ground."

embiggen, cromulent

DARYL, MARGOT, JESS, AND I were seated at Café Kopi Luwak enjoying our cups of espresso, compresso, represso, and corretto with some crumbly cakes. Daryl was showing us some pictures on his iPad. "Let me embiggen that detail," he said, dragging his fingers in opposite directions across the surface.

"*Embiggen?*" Margot said, her voice fairly dripping.

"It's a perfectly cromulent word," Jess said.

Margot was clearly about to say "*Cromulent?*" but decided to fight one villain at a time. "*Em, big, en.* The word is *enlarge.* Or *magnify. Expand.*"

"Well, you obviously understood it," Daryl said. "Besides, those words all have different nuances of meaning. And they're all less fun."

"They're better formed," Margot said. "*Embiggen* has a Latin prefix stuck onto an Anglo-Saxon root and suffix."

"Like *enlighten,*" I pointed out.

"But you can't just make a word up on the spot like that," Margot protested.

"I didn't," Daryl said. "Look." He held up the iPad. "That was the detail. It's a sign with the town motto of Springfield, from *The Simpsons*: 'A noble spirit embiggens the smallest man.'"

Margot was momentarily nonplussed.

"The word was coined in 1996 by writer Dan Greaney," Daryl added.

"It's perfidiously ugly," Margot said finally. "And unnecessary."

"So?" Jess, Daryl, and I all said at the same time. And we added, again in unison, "It's a perfectly cromulent word."

"*Cromulent!*" Margot said, turning to her next foe. "Is there really such a word?"

"Yes," Jess said.

"Since 1996," I added.

"It was invented by David X. Cohen, for *The Simpsons*," Daryl explained.

"That doesn't make it a real word!" Margot exclaimed.

Daryl was doing a quick Google search. "Well… over a quarter of a million usages might do it."

"But what does it mean?"

"I'd say its most common use is as a linguistic equivalent of *truthy*," Jess said. "Used for a neologism that has good feel and seems like it ought to be a real word."

"It does have a broader, plainer sense," Daryl said. "For instance, as Principal Skinner said, 'He's embiggened that role with his cromulent performance.' So 'valid' or 'credible' or something like that."

"To me," I said, "it has an air of something you can sink your teeth into. Like this coffee cake. Only transferred metaphorically."

"You mean with the taste of *crumble* and *granular* and the grabbiness of *grommet* and *glom*?" Jess asked.

"Yeah," I said. "And *succulent* and *corpulent* and *crapulent* and *esculent* and *opulent* and *poculent* and…"

"And *fraudulent* and *purulent* and *feculent* and *morbulent*," Margot grumbled.

"And *truculent*," Jess added.

"And *soylent green*!" Daryl said.

"Well," Margot said snarkily, "just because *u lent* a word to the language doesn't mean we must *cram* it in."

"Oh, there's infinite room to embiggen the vocabulary," Jess said.

Margot looked around as though contemplating defenestration. She slugged back the last of her coffee and declared, "I need a corretto."

I signalled the waitress. She came over. "What can I get you?"

"A round of corretti would be cromulent," I said.

She smiled. "Shall I embiggen them?"

Margot looked at her, slack-jawed. Pause. "Yeeeesss. Please."

epic

I WAS GIVING MONTGOMERY STARLING-BYRD, international president of the Order of Logogustation, and Grace Sherman, a noteworthy member from Mobile, Alabama, a tour around the Canadian National Exhibition. We had just entered the centre of deep-fried gravity, the Food Building, and I was pointing out some of the traditions and some of the splashy newcomers.

Montgomery read off the sign on one establishment that had a long line in front of it. "Epic Burgers and Waffles." He smirked. "I'm sure there's a long story behind that one." (An epic being, originally, a long verse form recounting heroic exploits – *The Iliad* and *The Odyssey* are two. From Greek ἔπος *epos* 'word, story, poem'.)

"Ah'm not cehtain ah can discern any rhyme or reason to it," Grace said, "although Ah must admit it looks vaguely familiah. We have burgers, and we have Krispy Kreme doughnuts, though Ah don't think Ah've seen anyone put them togethah befoah."

"Nor waffles and hamburgers, I think," Montgomery said. "Is this really an epic, or is it a comedy?"

"A farce, I think," I said, "since after eating it you will be, as the French say, *farci*" (stuffed). I did not mention that I had already eaten one of their donut burgers with egg and bacon. "I don't know whether this place has an official affiliation with Epic Meal Time, but they're certainly trading on the idea."

Montgomery arched an eyebrow. "Epic Meal Time? Is this a program whereon one watches heroes dine? Perhaps Odysseus's men making pigs of themselves at the table of Circe, or being eaten in turn by Polyphemus? Or Grendel crashing Hrothgar's feast?"

"It's a YouTube series wherein a band of antiheroes from Montreal make massive masculine meals of meat replete with endless quantities of bacon strips and large doses of Jack Daniels," I said. "The calorie count never fails to reach five digits."

"Ah wondah whethah Bertolt Brecht would have seen that as a worthy subject," Grace said. Brecht was a creator of what he called *epic theatre*, which aimed to focus more on actions and ideas and less on provoking the audience's emotional response. Massive overeating might have been a social reality worthy of his study, I mused.

Just then I saw something that made me flinch involuntarily.

Coming away from the counter at Epic Burgers was Marcus Brattle, my mentee, a stroppy 15-year-old of British extraction.

Not by himself. He was accompanied by a friend who appeared to have lately lost fights with a nail gun and a lawnmower. The friend was carrying a portable stereo and a video camera.

Marcus was carrying, under one arm, a skateboard, and in the other hand, an épée. The épée had, skewered on it, what appeared to be one of every deep-fried thing sold in the building – peanut-butter-and-jelly sandwich, mac and cheese, Oreos, Mars bar, fudge, and a variety of other things you didn't even think anyone could deep-fry – along with a donut burger, a Behemoth burger, and an American smashburger freshly bought.

I hesitated for a moment, caught between wanting to keep him from meeting Montgomery and Grace and a morbid fascination with what youthful idiocy he was embarked upon. The latter held sway long enough for him to see me. "Oh, hullo, Mentor!" he shouted.

"Well," said Montgomery to me, "it seems that you, too, are a character from an epic. And this must be your Telemachus."

I glanced at the video camera. "Tele-masochist, perhaps," I said. I turned to Marcus. "Marcus, this is Montgomery Starling-Byrd and Grace Sherman."

Marcus waggled the épée towards his accomplice. "This is Jason."

"Anothah epic hero," Grace observed.

"This will totally be epic!" Jason proclaimed.

"Well," Montgomery observed drily, "at least today's youth are focused on enterprises of great pith and moment. So much better than those who wanted to be 'radical,' or 'wicked,' or merely 'sick.'"

"If he's planning to eat all that," Grace said, "Ah do believe he will be sick."

144

"I am not only going to eat this," Marcus said, "I am going to do so while riding my skateboard. I am going to start right there –" he gestured at the nearby east door of the building – "and go down the steps and then career my way through the midway, not stopping until all is consumed."

Montgomery, Grace, and I all looked at each other. None of us could resist watching what was bound to become a crashing feast of its own. We followed him to the door.

"Cue epic music!" Marcus shouted. Jason pressed a button on the portable stereo and the opening of Orff's *Carmina Burana*, that archetypal music to declare the occurrence of an event for the ages, poured forth: "O! For! tu! naaa!" Marcus started off.

To our amazement, he cleared the steps on his skateboard without crashing, Jason running after him. He then proceeded off the sidewalk and started eating the donut burger while attempting to weave between the people. I ran after, while Grace and Montgomery maintained a more stately pace.

After about 20 metres, an execution flaw made itself evident: the bottom half of the donut burger fell off. Marcus, in trying to reach for it as it went, batted it down under the wheels of his skateboard. This resulted in abrupt loss of control, which sent him careering not down the midway but into a carnival game featuring bowling balls and more Smurfs than you have ever seen. The momentum carried Marcus through the players and into the Smurfs, and he flailed to a rest with a small Smurf stuffed in his mouth, his épée piercing a large Smurf, and nearly a hundred dollars' worth of fat and starch redecorating the surrounding Smurfs.

I am happy to report that Jason caught it all on video.

Quite the accomplishment, as he was laughing his head off.

"Epic fail, sir!" Jason shouted between howls of laughter.

"Épée flail," I countered.

Marcus spat out the small Smurf. "Epic? It's a tragedy!"

Grace and Montgomery had arrived at a trot. "Now, *that*," Grace declared, "is not a tragedy. He may have hubris and hamartia, but *that* is a farce!" She gestured at the stuffed creatures.

"But how the mighty have fallen," Montgomery said, his smirk displaying an unseemly schadenfreude. "If in something of a shorter time than it took Beowulf."

"O fortuna," I said.

"Tuna," Jason gasped between laughs, "may be the only thing that Grandpa Smurf is not wearing now."

Marcus grabbed the remains of a burger and took a bite. "Mentor," he said, eyeing the game operator, who was finally beginning to stop laughing, "I spent all my money on the food. I think I may need to borrow some."

beg the question, ad hominem

MY ANNUAL SPREE OF MASOCHISM — setting up a table for the Order of Logogustation at the Frosh Week of my local university — rolled around again this week. I always try to maintain a game face, and I usually get some nibbles, but more often I just gather anecdotes for telling later over alcohol.

Today I was at the table and there was a lean, angular young man standing in front of it, looking over the printed material a bit cagily. A young woman with a certain feline grace strolled up. "Logogustation," she said, pronouncing it correctly the first time. She looked further at the sign. "Word tasting."

"Words are delicious," I offered.

"That kind of begs the question," she said, "of whether words can be said to have taste at all."

The young man slapped down the brochure and exclaimed, "*No it does not!*" I jumped slightly; cat girl just raised an eyebrow. He continued. "It does not beg the question! That's not what *begging the question* means!"

"I know a lot of people who use it to mean exactly that," cat girl said.

"Well, they're wrong," he said. "It means assuming the point that's at issue. Trying to prove X with an argument that only works if X is true. Get it right."

The young woman drew back slightly and gave him an elevator look (top to toe and back). "You're using language as a weapon," she said. "You're deeply insecure and you feel that you can improve your self-image by belittling others. Actually it just makes you look worse."

"Oh, great," said angle boy. "You lose. The best you can muster is an ad hominem. That's pathetic."

"That's not an ad hominem," I said, doing what I could to suppress a smile at his error.

"She's attacking my character!" he said. "You're an idiot! Of course it's an ad hominem!"

"*Argumentum ad hominem* is the logical fallacy of asserting that a person's argument is flawed because of a flaw in a person's character," I said. "Or, conversely, asserting that a person's argument is good because of the person's good character. But she's not saying you're wrong because you're an unpleasant person. Her assertion regarding your character is a different level of analysis. She's not saying you're wrong at all. She's just saying that the way you're presenting your point reveals something important about your character. And that, pragmatically, your entry into the discourse may be serving a primary goal other than the ostensible one."

Cat girl considered this momentarily and smiled. "OK."

"I speak frankly," angle boy said overtop of her. "I'm just bluntly honest. And —" he turned to cat girl —"you're just standing there smiling, assassinating my character instead of answering my argument."

"Actually," she said, "it was meant as a helpful observation. And your statements about my character — and his —" she nodded in my direction — "are not germane to the argument. In fact, they would meet your definition of ad hominems."

"You see," angle boy said to me, "she looks like she's right because she's calm. And because I get worked up because it's important, I look like I'm wrong."

"It does make people less receptive," I said. "Of course it would be fallacious to say you're wrong because you're upset. Just as it's fallacious to use righteous indignation as proof of the validity of one's argument. I'm not sure if there's a proper name for that fallacy, but I'm inclined to call it *argumentum ad passionem*. Or *argumentum ad affectum*. It's all too common in political discourse."

"Just by the by," cat girl said to me, "what do *you* say about *begging the question?*"

"We-ell," I said, "the original meaning is indeed 'assuming the conclusion'. It's a bit of a dodgy translation of *petitio principii*. I prefer to avoid it because those people who are familiar with the original meaning tend to take exception to the more recent use."

Angle boy made a "you see" gesture with his hands. Cat girl cocked her head. "You taste words," she said. "So what does *begging the question* taste like?"

Ah, back on safer ground. "Everyone can taste words. Say it slowly: *begging the question*. What does it feel like?"

She ran it through her mouth a couple of times. "Blunt and withdrawn at the start. Then dry and thirsty on *question*."

"And what other words does it make you think of?"

Cat girl smiled a little. "*Big bad bugger bogeyman bagboy… quick quiz quirky quiet quest.*"

Angle boy interjected with some asperity, "Petitio principii. Stupidity."

"*Ad hominem*," I said.

"It is not!" he said.

"No," I said, "I mean taste it."

"Taste this," angle boy said and made a rude gesture. He added "What a bunch of bullshit" and walked away.

"Hmmm," cat girl said, apparently in response to my suggestion of *ad hominem*. "*A dominant, domineering, abominable… humbug.*"

I smiled and extended my hand. "James. Pleased to meet you."

She shook my hand. "Arlene." Then she picked up a membership brochure, made a little gesture of salutation with it and, putting it in her bag, said "See you later" and moved on.

Caerphilly

MONTGOMERY STARLING-BYRD, INTERNATIONAL PRESIDENT of the Order of Logogustation, happened to be passing through town and was pleased to have the chance to catch the Toronto Symphony Orchestra perform, among other things, William Walton's *Henry V* featuring Christopher Plummer, the Toronto Mendelssohn Choir, and the Toronto Children's Chorus. Today was the day before the first performance, and he was at Domus Logogustationis for conviviality with local word tasters. We had laid on some cheese and crackers and wine and so forth.

"I'll have to be off to the dress rehearsal soon," I said to Montgomery and to Maury, looking at my watch.

"Oh, yes," said Montgomery, "you sing with the choir. Well, sing carefully."

Elisa Lively was passing by. "You're singing in something?"

"Walton's *Henry the Fifth*," I said.

"Oh," she said, "can I see the score?"

"English two, French zero," Maury said. I reached down to my bag, pulled out my copy of the score, and handed it to her.

She flipped through it. "There's quite a lot of tacet here."

"Orchestra and narrator," I said.

She kept flipping. "Oh, the Agincourt carol, nice." Flip, flip. At the last page, she read a line at the bottom and remarked, "The layout was done in Caerphilly." She pronounced the place name "*care*-filly."

"Say that carefully," Montgomery said. "The stress is on the second syllable."

"Ker-*fil*ly," she said.

"Now, when I hear that," Maury said, "I think of cheese."

"I'm certain the performance will not be cheesy," Montgomery said.

"Because of Philly cream cheese?" Elisa asked.

150

"No," Maury said, "Caerphilly is a kind of hard, crumbly white cheese. Named after the town it was first made in."

"And the town's name," Montgomery said, "means 'Ffili's fort'."

"Where is that, anyway?" Elisa asked.

"It's a suburb of Cardiff," Montgomery said, "down in south Wales. It is known for Caerphilly Castle, an excellent, almost archetypal example of the medieval castle. Thirteenth century, built for military purposes."

"I daresay the English would have had a harder time attacking that than they did attacking Harfleur," I remarked, referring to the first battle in Shakespeare's *Henry V*, on which Walton's piece is based. "They'd look at it and go once more into their breeches."

Montgomery raised one eyebrow slightly at my off-colour pun on a Shakespearean quote. Then he said, "They would certainly have to do it carefully. But in fact, although it was built by English to intimidate the Welsh – at which it succeeded – the English did attack it too. Well, one set of English did it against another: the castle's last real battle was when Queen Isabella besieged it in the early 1300s as an attack on her husband, Edward the Second, and his favourite, Hugh le Despenser."

"It would have been either ironic or fitting," Maury said, "for Henry to attack it, for though he was an English king, he was, as he declares in Shakespeare's play, a Welshman."

"Well," I said, looking at my watch again, "today is St. Crispin's Day." (That's the day of the battle of Agincourt.)

"Tomorrow, rather," Montgomery said.

"October 25, in reality," Maury said.

"Well, today is 'have some crispies day,'" Elisa said, and handed Montgomery a crispy cracker with a large dollop of cream cheese on it. "Be careful – that's Philly."

"You seem to have it in ample quantities," Montgomery said.

"Oh, yes," Elisa said. "We have a huge dispenser." She snort-guffawed at her pun.

I made a small salute as I sidled towards the door. "Hold down the fort," I said.

"And hold up the *forte*," Montgomery said. "I'll see you on the morrow." And with that I left.

151

crisp

THE *HENRY V* CONCERT was over, and I met up with Montgomery Starling-Byrd on the sidewalk outside Roy Thomson Hall.

"How was it?" I said.

"Crisp," he said.

"As in Crispin or Crispinian?" These two were the martyred twin brothers honoured on St. Crispin's Day, October 25, which is when Henry V won the battle of Agincourt. You may be interested to know that the brothers lived in Soissons, France, less than 300 km away from Agincourt (take the highway A26), but 1130 years before the battle.

"Yes," he said. "Aside from the martyrdom bit."

"No martyrdom for Crispus today," I said. "I'm not wearing a tux." I'll explain that one: Crispin and Crispinian are derived from Latin *crispus*, which means "curly"; Crispus Attucks, a man of half-African and half-Wampanoag ancestry, is generally thought of as the first person killed in the American Revolution, at the Boston Massacre. And, yes, I was wearing white tie and tails, not black tie and tuxedo.

"Indeed, proper tails are a constant." I suspect he was making a joke on Emperor Constantine I, who had a son named Crispus. Whom he had killed.

"Just as well," I said, "my tux is going to hell in a handbasket." That was a pun on Helena, the mother of Constantine, and also on Helena Bonham-Carter, cousin of Crispin Bonham-Carter, who is also an actor.

"Well, let us turn back to the future for a moment," Montgomery said. I was surprised that he had seen *Back to the Future*, which starred Crispin Glover as McFly. "I ought to have gone once more into the breach in the concert hall; my intermission libations are catching up on me. Is there a pay toilet around here?"

"No pay toilets in Toronto," I said. "We prefer to hold our manhoods cheap – or free, actually." This was a reference to a line in King

Henry's speech before the battle. "We could go across King Street to a pub – I'll have a pint, and you'll have a –"

"Yes," Montgomery said, cutting me off, "that sounds good. A snack perhaps. All I've had is a packet of crisps. I wonder whether they have crêpes." Yes, *crêpe* is cognate with *crisp* too. We started walking.

"More likely just French fries," I said. "Calamari and Guinness are what I usually get. They might have curly fries, though."

"Indeed, the original crisps," Montgomery said. What he meant, of course, was that, as I've mentioned, *crisp* comes from Latin *crispus* – yes, 'curly' – and came to mean 'rippled, wrinkled' in the 1300s and 'brittle' only in the 1500s. Lexicographers are unsure how it came to have the 'brittle' meaning but speculate that the sound of the word had some influence. "But of course," Montgomery added, "French fries are really chips, looking like wood chips. Whereas you colonials use *chips* to refer to crisps."

"I do admit," I said, "potato chips sound more like crisps. You can hear it when you eat them: 'crisp, crisp, crisp.'" We walked on for a few seconds, pondering onomatopoeia. "So," I said, returning to the original topic, "Crisp – I mean, Christopher Plummer was suitably plummy for you?"

"He has a voice one can curl up with," Montgomery said. "And the orchestra and the two choirs could make one's hair curl. And it was all, as I said, crisp and clear."

"Marvellous," I said. "I'm looking forward to doing it again on Saturday. But now," I said, veering to the steps to the pub, "let it be in our flowing cups freshly rememb'red."

whereabouts

THE ORDER OF LOGOGUSTATION'S monthly Words, Wines, and Whatever tasting event was drawing to a close. One of our newest members, Arlene, was looking at the chairs around the room.

"Inventorying our assets?" I said.

"It's more about something to wear," she said. "My jacket. Its exact present whereabouts are unknown."

"Magnificent," I said. "You've managed to include three of the top collocations for *whereabouts*: *unknown, present,* and *exact.*"

"True," she said. "People seldom say that whereabouts are known."

"In fact," I said, "if you Google 'whereabouts are known' you get the suggestion 'whereabouts are unknown'. Interestingly, if you Google 'whereabouts *is* known' you get no suggestion and far fewer hits – about fifteen percent as many. The same *is/are* proportion holds for *unknown,* but with about ten times as many hits."

"Well, why would anyone say *whereabouts is*?" Very brief pause. "I suspect I'm about to find out."

I was smiling. "It's not a plural."

"Of course not," she said, looking heavenward. "Why should I assume something is a plural just because it looks like one?"

"The *s* is a survival of the genitive from when it was used to form adverbs – *besides, anyways, towards,* and so on."

She looked at me through the tops of her glasses. "Survival of the genitive. Sounds like linguistic Darwinism."

"Except in language some words and phrases persist long after their environment has changed to one unsuited to them."

"Well, I'm unsuited for the environment outside," she said. "If I don't find something to wear about now, I will lack the wherewithal to get home comfortably, no ifs, ands, or buts." She continued moving through the chairs. I could see her begin to roll the word around in her mouth silently as she did so: *where-a-bout-s.* Then she stopped

154

and turned again to me. "So I could actually say 'Whereabouts is my jacket'?"

"Exactly," I said. "That was its first use: as a long way of saying 'where' or a short way of saying 'in what area'. Sort of like *whatever* versus *what*."

"Which means," she said, "I could also say 'My jacket's where is unknown.'"

"True, although since we generally no longer devoice the *wh*, there is risk of confusion."

"Well, there we are," she said. "I am confused about the exact present where of my wear."

"Yes, the whereabouts of what you will wear about outside is unknown."

Jess came up to us. "I don't know about that," she said.

I raised an eyebrow. "You're disagreeing with my syntax?"

"Your semantics," she said. "Its whereabouts may be unknown to you, but they are not – sorry, it is not – to me." She held up a jacket.

"Oh!" said Arlene. "Whereabouts was it?"

"Hanging off a cupboard in the kitchen," Jess said, "but wherefore I know not."

nevertheless, nonetheless, notwithstanding

JESS HELD UP ARLENE'S JACKET, which had been missing.

"Oh!" said Arlene. "Whereabouts was it?"

"Hanging off a cupboard in the kitchen," Jess said, "but wherefore I know not."

"*Wherefore...* Is that short for *what it was there for*?" Arlene said playfully. "How did it get there? Nevertheless, I am glad you found it."

"Oh!" I said, a lightbulb going on in my head. "When you arrived a bit early we conscripted you immediately into helping bring food and beverage out. We took you into the kitchen and you left your jacket there."

"Oh yes," Arlene said, "notwithstanding I was the newbie..."

"Especially because you were the newbie," I said. "And how do you get involved? Not with standing around waiting!"

"Well, carrying trays of food, I felt like a waiter nonetheless," Arlene said. "Although, as I know from working for a caterer, they also wait who stand and serve."

Jess was shaking her head in amusement and mild amazement. "Where did you find her, James?"

"Not without standing around," I said. "Manning the table at frosh week can be a bit dodgy, but nevertheless there's always the more."

"And nonetheless there's one the more, at least this time," Arlene said. "Those are nice long words that don't say a whole lot, aren't they? *Nevertheless, nonetheless, nothwithstanding...* insofar as they say anything at all, it's just 'but' or 'although'."

"I believe medieval English law clerks got paid by the letter," I said.

"Well, not by the word," Jess said. "Otherwise why concatenate so?"

"Are these words really that old?" Arlene said.

"Older, even," I said. "Especially earlier versions of them such as *netheless* and *natheless*, which come from Old English, before the years were in triple digits. The phrases got used adverbially so much that they got treated as single words. We don't use *natheless* anymore because we don't use *na* anymore, but *none* and the now-archaic use of *never the* and *never a* to mean 'not' have taken over."

"We use *natheless* nevermore!" Arlene said.

"I think she's raven," Jess quipped.

"Just as we use *neverthemore* nevermore," I said, "but it was a word in use at one time, to mean 'definitely not'."

"And *nevermore* means 'no longer', as does *not anymore*," Arlene said, thinking it through, "so they refer to something that stopped. The converse would be something that hasn't stopped... *Still*."

"Yes," Jess said, "if something hasn't stopped still, it still hasn't stopped. I love how we use *still* for something that keeps moving. And is therefore not still."

"Well, what would it still be there for?" I said.

"What are these words still there for, if we have shorter ones that serve?" Arlene said. "Nevertheless they are, their length notwithstanding."

"Ah, multiple morphemes are the morphine of pompous parlance," I said. "If we wish to be more formal and authoritative, we often drag in confections of multiple Latin and French bits, but these ones are made of Anglo-Saxon bits: *never, the, less*; *not* plus *withstanding*, which is *with* on *standing*, which is *stand* plus *ing*."

"Notwithstanding that *notwithstanding* is probably based on Latin *non obstante*," Jess said. "Still, we could say it at even greater length: 'It is no less the case that it is so' rather than 'Nevertheless, it is so,' or 'All of the preceding does not present an obstacle' rather than 'All of the preceding notwithstanding.' But you're right, the longer words are like verbal truncheons, and the longer ones hit harder. However," she said, dropping into a chair, "if we're going to keep on this tack, it will not be without sitting down."

"Notwithstanding that it sounds like fun," I said, "my system and my spouse will not withstand a lack of sleep. Enough morphemes, more morpheus for me."

"And now I have my wherewithal," Arlene said, putting on her jacket, "something to wear with all the words in my head and the winds outside…"

"I hope it will be withstanding the winds," Jess said. "It's a bit breezy out there."

"And in here," Arlene said, and smiled. "I'll see you later." And with that she breezed out.

mondegreen

IT WAS CLEANING-UP TIME after yet another lively word tasting at Domus Logogustationis, and our own especially lively word taster, Elisa Lively, was in the kitchen doing the wash-up while a few of the rest of us gathered dishes and brought them in.

I came in with a stack of bowls, set them down next to the sink. Elisa was sudsed up the elbows and singing Deep Purple's "Smoke on the Water" happily:

"Slow-motion Walter, the fire engine guy…"

I choked back a guffaw, pretended it was a cough, and headed back out. (The real words are "Smoke on the water and fire in the sky.") Presently I returned with a stack of plates. She had switched to Abba:

"See that girl, watch her scream, kicking the dancing queen…"

I paused for a split second, goggled, set the plates and retreated. (The original words are "See that girl, watch that scene, dig in the dancing queen.") I gathered an assortment of wine glasses, including my own nearly empty one, shouldered the swinging kitchen door open and headed back in. Just as I was tossing back the last of my Zinfandel, I clicked in to her rendition of Robert Palmer's "Addicted to Love":

"You might as well face it, you're a dick with a glove."

I did what in the comedy business is known as a spit take. That is to say, I sprayed my Zinfandel across the tile floor and commenced coughing. I barely managed to set the glasses down without demolishing them.

Elisa turned, solicitous. She reached for a jug on the counter and poured me a glass. And with it she started in on Led Zeppelin's "Whole Lotta Love":

"You need Kool-Aid, baby I'm not fooling…"

I held up my hand and coughed and gasped and finally managed to swallow a bit of the Kool-Aid. "Good grief," I said, "were you tasting *mondegreen* tonight?"

"Mondegreen?" Elisa said, fetching a mop. "No, I stuck with the Kool-Aid."

"No, I mean the word. *Mondegreen.* I'll take that as a no."

"I don't think I've heard it," Elisa said. "It sounds kind of like a cheese. Or maybe a country – no, that's Montenegro. Is it related to *verdigris?*"

"Not even to a fair degree," I said. "It comes from a mishearing by the writer Sylvia Wright. When she was a kid, she enjoyed hearing her mother read from Percy's *Reliques,* and the first stanza, by her hearing, ended 'The hae slain the Earl Amurray / And Lady Mondegreen.' But actually it was 'the Earl O' Moray / And laid him on the green.' So in 1954 Wright published an article in *Harper's* in which she gave such mishearings the name *mondegreens.*"

"Oh!" said Elisa. "Like when I was a kid and I sang in church about 'gladly the cross-eyed bear' – and every Christmas I'd sing 'Good tidings we bring to you and your thing.'"

"Exactly," I said. "Mishearings, typically funny, of song lyrics. Often they're actually less plausible than the real lyrics. I don't remember making any really funny mistakes, but I remember hearing Boney M's 'Rasputin' and thinking the line 'Russia's greatest love machine' was 'Rickashane a slokashi,' some kind of imitation Russian. It really says something about the human brain, the things we'll fill in when we can't quite make out the words. Sort of like the weird things we see in the dark – why would we think what we're seeing is a house plant when it could so easily be a four-foot spider?"

"Well, *Mondegreen* does sound like a reasonable name," Elisa said. "It has two recognizable parts, with the *monde* like from French for 'world'. It's like some... relic from a green world!"

"Or from the salad days of the listener, when she was green in judgement. We do have lots of words with *m* and *nd*, like *mandate, mend, mind, Monday, mundungus...*"

"Green Monday," Elisa said. "Isn't *Mundungus* just a name from Harry Potter?"

"Also a word for bad tobacco. Green mundungus would really be nasty, I'm sure."

"Mondo bizarro," Elisa said, possibly agreeing. "But speaking of salad... there's some you could help put away." She opened a cupboard to reveal a bunch of plastic containers suited for the task, and sang out, as from Nirvana's "Smells Like Teen Spirit," "Here we are now, in containers." (It's really "Here we are now, entertain us.")

I smiled. As I started scooping some Waldorf salad into one of the containers, I started in a version of Toto's "Africa" (the refrain of which really goes "Gonna take a lot to take me away from you / There's nothing that a hundred men or more could ever do / I bless the rains down in Africa..."): "Gonna take a lot to take me away from food..."

Elisa added the next line: "There's nothing that a hundred men on Mars could ever do."

We sang together, her washing, me scooping: "I left my brains down in Africa..."

littoral

"YOU WERE NOT PLEASED with your Caribbean sojourn?" I said. Marica and Ronald had just returned from a vacation and seemed disaffected.

"The resort was a literal garbage dump," Ronald said.

"Rubbish everywhere," Marica said. "Not just littoral. Riparian, pelagic, probably even benthic, for all I know." For once they had the illusion of being in the same conversation.

"Probably been thick on the ground for a long time, yeah" Ronald said.

"Benthic on the ground?" Marica said, and appeared to be about to say "that doesn't make sense." She paused instead. "...Oh. Never mind."

"I mean, for her, a beach is a literary thing," Ronald said. "A place to read a book. But I like to look at the glitter all over the waves, the little roll of the small boats on the sea, the flutter of birds, the rattle of scattering pebbles and the skittering of little critters... a lotta real nice things like that. I can hardly enjoy that when there's litter all over the place," he concluded bitterly.

"Oh, it matters to me too," Marica said. "Environment is important. The littoral zone is not just a tourist attraction; it's essential to the planet's health."

Ronald snorted. "Yeah, the zone of literal reality would be kinda important. Even if some people prefer the figurative."

Marica looked at Ronald over the rims of her glasses. "L. I. T T. O. R. A L. *Littoral.* 'Of or pertaining to the zone including the shore of an ocean or lake.'" She turned to me. "Why the hell don't we pronounce it 'litTORal,' anyway? That would be so much less ambiguous."

"Less fun, too," I said. "Sometimes. But the stress pattern seems to have been set in Latin with the original root *litus*, 'shore', which had a long first vowel and so was stressed on the first syllable. I do like how it causes the tongue to touch the tip, then roll back and forward to touch again, like a wave at the shore. The *l*'s are the high water, the *t*'s halfway down, the *r* the low water…"

"I suppose," Marica mused, "we could see the littoral zone as like the interface between the great seas of imagination, with their ships of fiction, and the solid world of physical reality. The literal littoral zone."

"The littered littoral zone," Ronald said. "The only crabs were me and Marica."

"So your vacation was a washout? Obliterated?"

"No, we salvaged it by shifting to another resort farther up the shore."

Marica nodded. "A littoral lateral relocation."

sketchy

"WELL," SAID MAURY, "IT WAS ALL a bit sketchy."

"Seedy, you mean? Unpleasant?" I said. Maury was telling me about his blind date of the night before.

"No, it's just that we hadn't made very detailed plans. I suppose I was a touch skittish. So we had no clear picture of where to go."

"Where did you meet up with her?"

"At a coffee shop in the west end. I wasn't sure what to expect – the description of her was rather sketchy."

"I'm going to assume you don't mean disreputable."

"Correct. Our mutual friend said she looked vaguely like Christina Ricci. But she had said she would have a Gucci bag and a crutch, so she was easy to spot."

"A crutch?"

"She said she's a soccer coach, and caught a kick in the shin. But this also meant we chose somewhere not too far to walk. Neither of us had been to the place, but it looked fetching, in a sketchy way."

"I don't usually eat at sketchy places…"

"No," Maury said, "I meant the décor. It was a touch kitschy, but the walls were covered in sketches and etchings of bocce players."

"Italian food, then?"

"That's what the menu said. Well, the details were sketchy, but, then, so, as it turned out, was the food."

"Your food was lacking in definition?"

"No, it was dodgy. Wretched, in fact. They called it chicken cacciatore, but what came out of their kitchen was scorched and botched and drenched with ketchup."

"Oh, dear."

"She found a good excuse for ditching the joint. She said her leg under the cast was getting itchy and she wanted to go home and do some tai chi to make it feel better. I was invited to join her, or anyway to sip a Scotch and watch."

"Um," I said. "*That* almost sounds sketchy."

"It was an acceptable proposition in a clutch. I *was* a bit surprised that she lived nearby."

"Why?"

"Well, the neighbourhood is rather sketchy in my mind."

"Huh. Usually you look things up and get to know the details…"

"No," Maury said, "I mean that to my knowledge it's a seedy area. At every corner there was a clutch of sketchy characters. But her place was nonetheless quite nice, not dicey at all."

"So how did it go from there?"

"She marched me into her kitchen and poured me a Scotch, then dropped the crutch. As I reached for it, she made a switcheroo."

"Your drink?"

"No – with a quick rip, she undid the stretchy velcro on the cast and fetched me a swift kick in the tush. Not brutish, just a little wicked. And shouted 'Gotcha!'"

"Whoa."

"It turns out she's a bit of a joker – a kittenish character. And she uses the cast on blind dates to have some control over the situation. If it gets touchy, she can just back out. Or if she wants it to get touchy, she can do what in fact she did."

"So how was the rest?"

"Sketchy, I'm afraid."

"Uh-oh."

"No, sorry, I just mean that I had too much Scotch and I can't put together a complete picture. I believe I had fun. There was some opera involved. A CD of *Gianni Schicchi*, if my recollection is accurate. Rather catchy, as a matter of fact." He sang a snatch of a well-known aria: "*O mio babbino caro*…" He coughed.

"You were singing along? Your voice sounds a little scratchy."

"It has been scotched."

"You *are* looking a little under the weather, actually. Just a bit, ah…"

Maury nodded and rubbed his head. "…Sketchy, yes."

pie

DARYL EMERGED FROM THE KITCHEN of Domus Logogustationis holding two fresh, steaming pies. He plunked them down on a table and said, "There!"

"Well, aren't you sweet as pie!" Elisa Lively exclaimed. "What's the occasion?"

"Pie Day!" he said, or so it sounded.

"Proto-Indo-European Day?" Maury said, referring to the reconstructed proto-language commonly abbreviated as PIE. "Are these made with roots?" I, meanwhile, had started to sing "Pie day, pie day" in emulation of Rebecca Black. "Please stop," Maury said in my general direction.

"It's March fourteenth," Daryl said. "Three fourteen. Pi is three point one four."

"Which would mean," I said, "that pi second was at 1:59:26 – point 5." I had always known that memorizing pi in my childhood would come in handy sometime.

"I think I don't follow," Elisa said.

"Pi," I said. "3.1415926535897932384626…" Daryl joined in after a few digits and we recited in unison until Elisa started waving her hands and said, "What are you doing? Stop."

"Pi in your face!" Daryl said.

"All I know is pi r squared," Elisa said.

"These pie are round," Maury observed. "You can tell by the circumference: these two pie are."

"If no one else is going to," I said, "I'm going into the kitchen to get plates and forks and serving implements."

"No need," said Jess, emerging from the kitchen with the requisites. "Easy as pie."

"Well, hi, cutie pie," Elisa said.

"There's another mathematical formula," I said. "Visual appeal as the product of quality, time, and the amount of pie you eat: $qt\pi$. Proof that dessert is good for your looks."

"Keep it on the q.t.," Jess said. "Looks good to me," Elisa said at the same time.

"Well, dig in," Daryl said. "There's ample pie."

"I'll have a sample of pie, then," Maury said, reaching for a knife.

"Apple pie?" Elisa said.

"And bumbleberry pie," Daryl said.

"Better bumble than humble," I said, taking a plate from the stack Jess had set down. "I'll be trying both pies. I like to have a finger in every pie."

"Don't put your finger in these ones," Daryl said. I launched into a snippet from Pink Floyd's "Money": "Share it fairly but don't take a slice of my pie." And I took a slice of each pie.

"Perhaps we can have some pies in quiet," Jess said, and added – at me – "Chatter-pie."

"Nice shirt," I said to Jess. "How would you describe the colour… badger-pie?" Jess stuck her tongue out at me.

Maury looked at my two-pie-piece plate. "You would have taken one of each even had there been four, wouldn't you?"

"At least one, yes," I said, and took a bite. "Mmm. Yummy."

He nodded. "You really are a magpie."

"Pies for the pie," I said. More for the benefit of Elisa and perhaps Daryl – Maury and Jess probably knew this – I added, "Magpies were originally called *pies*, from Latin *pica*. The *mag* was added perhaps in the same way as adding *Jack* to *daw* – it seems to be from *Maggie*."

"So did someone bake four-and-twenty of them in a pie some time?" Elisa asked between bites.

I almost started singing "Pie-pie blackbird," but thought better of it. "No one's entirely sure where *pie* for the dish came from," I said, eyeing the pies, "but it dates from after *pie* for the bird, and the first ones were made of a variety of savoury things and meats, so it might have been a magpie-style collection. But that's speculation. Perhaps with further research…"

"You'll get pie in the sky when you die," Jess said, echoing the cynical line that originated the phrase *pie in the sky*.

"As long as I could have it with a nice glass of port," I said.

"And get thoroughly pie-eyed?" Maury said.

"Why not," I said. "Make the pie higher!"

guys

I WAS SITTING IN the usual coffee spot with Margot and Jess when Arlene Chu, one of our newer student members, walked in with some friends. She spotted us and turned to her friends. "Hang on, guys, I'm just going to say hi over here."

Margot was her usual charming self. "Your friends are guys?" she said as Arlene approached.

"Huh? No, they're all female."

"That's what I thought," Margot said, "but you called them *guys*. I thought perhaps they were in dis-*guys*." Yes, she said it so as to highlight the pun.

"I'd say," said Jess, "it's just because they're anonymous."

"Anonymity does not confer a sex change," Margot said primly.

"I think you've been out-Fawksed," I said to Margot. Jess gave me a thumbs-up.

"Wait," said Arlene. "You're referring to how members of the hacker group Anonymous wear Guy Fawkes masks."

"Very good!" Jess said. "Yes, as inspired by the movie *V for Vendetta*."

"But all those Guys are guys," Margot said.

"A woman may wear a mask," Arlene said. "And words can mask gender too."

"Interestingly," I said, "though words can be evocative, this word, in the vocative – the plural vocative – is less specific than in its other senses. It is indeed a guise. A group of females are not guys, and are unlikely to be called *the guys*, but they can still be addressed as *guys* or *you guys*."

"Our tongue is losing its specificity," Margot said.

"Not always a bad thing," Jess said. "One's sex is not necessarily pertinent in all occasions. But I think this one has its roots in loss of number specificity a longer time ago. Once we started using *you* for all second persons and dropped the singular familiar *thou* altogether, we lost a good way of making it clear whether we were addressing one or many."

"And *you all* sounds a little too Southern for many people's tastes," I added.

"We got along fine until just recently," Margot said.

"How recent is recent?" I said. "When I was a kid in the '70s, there was a magazine and TV show called *The Electric Company* – for kids who had outgrown *Sesame Street*. On it, there was a character, Millie the Helper, played by Rita Moreno, who would shout to a group of no-matter-what sex, 'Hey you guys!'"

"For mixed-sex groups, perhaps," said Margot, "consistent with the use of the male for any case where sex is not known..." Jess, Arlene, and I all rolled our eyes.

"It's useful and it's entrenched now," Jess said, "at least in casual usage. After *Legally Blonde* and the sorority girls saying things like 'Oh my God, you guys' to each other, it's a done deal. Women, especially young women, tend to be the cynosures of linguistic change."

"So anyway," Arlene said, "to make sure I have this straight: this old Anglo-Norman name happened to be the name of a guy – ha, literally a Guy – who tried to blow up parliament, and was hanged for real and then ever thereafter in effigy, and from those effigies *Guy* came to be a term for a grotesque or frightful or odd-looking man, and from that it transferred to a general term for a male. And now, just when you're using it to address a group in the plural, it can refer to males or females."

"Semantic bleaching," Margot said with some asperity.

"Well," Arlene said, "at least Fawkes's first name wasn't *Dick*."

"Couldn't be worse than *Guy*, could it?" Margot said.

Arlene's friends had reached the front of the line and were calling to her for her order. She started to walk away. "OK, well, 'bye, you guys, nice chatting." She paused and said to Margot, "'Bye, you dick." And stuck her tongue out and went on her way.

170

expletive

I WAS BACK AT the house of Marcus Brattle, my adolescent ex-Brit mentee, tutoring him in the finer (and sometimes coarser) points of grammar.

"One thing I've always wondered," he said. "In a sentence like *It's raining*, what's the *it*? The sky, the weather, what?"

"None of the above," I said. "It's just there because in English we need an explicit subject. It's just a filler. An expletive."

"A wot?"

"Expletive." I wrote it down so he could see the spelling.

"Oh," he said, "ex-*plee*-tive. As in deleted."

"In North America," I said, "it is pronounced *ex*-pla-tive. In spite of the fact that the *ex* is a prefix. It's from *ex* 'out' and *plere* 'fill'."

"Right enough," Marcus said. "I've said a few expletives when I've had to fill some things out. But, to return to the first question, I didn't say 'It's bloody raining,' I just said 'It's raining.'"

"Yes, the *it* is an expletive."

"You're missing a 'sh.'"

Pause. I sighed. "Not 'Shit's raining.'"

"For which let us be thankful," Marcus said. "That would be excretive." Some days I wondered whether I had succeeded in teaching him anything other than my own worst habits. "And perhaps explosive," he added.

I waved that one away with both hands. "Well, let me be explicative. *Expletive* refers to all sorts of verbal padding and empty filler."

"Things that may be well deleted."

"If they're emphatic vulgarities, they may be trimmed without grammatical damage. Note that not all vulgarities are really expletives; some are main verbs and nouns."

"No shit. You're shitting me."

"Two good examples."

171

"Thank you. I will accept the bonus points." Marcus smiled.

"Anyway," I continued, "syntactic expletives such as the subjects of *It's raining* and *There's a duck on the table* are there precisely because they can't be deleted. In a complete English sentence, you need a subject to receive the nominative case from the verb." I stopped, realizing that case theory was probably a bit beyond the curriculum. "They're spear-carriers," I said.

"Well, you can't shake a spear at that, but it sounds a bit exploitative."

I nodded. "Theirs is an empty existence."

"I like the sound of it, though... *expletive*." He said with with drawn-out relish. "It sounds excellent and complicated. Crisp and clicky and mechanical, rather like the sound of some of the naughty words it refers to, with their 'sh' and 'f' and 't' and 'k' and so on. Actually," he said, getting up, "I think I know what it sounds like." He trotted into the kitchen. "How's this?" I heard a sound that was evidently a cultery or utensil drawer being rattled.

"Sort of like that," I said.

"No, no, wait for it..." he shouted. There was a sound as of pots and pans being banged around. "I think it sounds like an egg being cracked into a frying pan."

Oh brother. Adolescent boy. Another excuse for a snack. I got up and headed into the kitchen. Where I promptly collided with Marcus, on his way between fridge and stove. "Bollocks!" he said, stepping back.

"Now that," I said, "was an exclamative expletive."

"Actually," he said, indicating the yellow-and-clear goo and shell bits now running down the front of my shirt, "that was an egg-*splative*."

leveret, levirate

A FEW OF US were lounging around in Domus Logogustationis (the local headquarters of the Order of Logogustation), mostly reading, occasionally exchanging comments on various words.

Elisa Lively looked up from her book. "What's a levirate?"

"A leveret?" said Maury, barely glancing up from his magazine. "A young hare." He returned to his reading.

"Oh, thanks," Elisa said. Pause while she looked back at her book. "Huh." Another pause. "Huh." She looked up again. "Because this book uses the term all the time but doesn't define it. But that doesn't really clear things up all that much. Young hair."

"No?" Maury looked over the top of his magazine and peered over at Elisa's book, but the title of it was not visible at his angle. "There are some other senses based on that, though they are not really in current use."

"Such as?"

"Oh, a spiritless person. Or a mistress."

"Oh. That must be what it is. Hm." Another pause. "So a levirate is a mistress because of the link between hair and tresses?"

"Hair and..." Maury was fleetingly confused, and then realized the confusion, or at least part of it. "*Hare* as in like a rabbit. *H-a-r-e*."

"But... so... OK. I thought maybe it was some kind of game or an instrument or something. But I can see some relation to keeping a mistress."

"Well, rabbits are a kind of game. As are hares. You can hunt them."

"But can you practise them?"

"Can you what?"

"I guess when they say *practise the levirate* they mean they're in the practice of keeping mistresses. I mean, I don't see where little animals really come into this."

173

"What *are* you reading?" Maury was straining forward in his seat trying to see the book. "I take it it's not lagomorphology." Elisa opened her mouth to ask a question, which Maury anticipated. "The study of rabbits, hares, and pikas, and such like."

"Oooh, I love pikas!" Elisa said. "But no, it's anthropology. They're talking about some cultures in New Guinea."

"They have hares there?"

"Well, the thing is, I thought maybe they were more interested in heirs. Because they've been talking about marital customs and widows and…"

Maury, finally cluing in, cut her off. "*Lee*-virate! That," he said, holding his finger in the air, "is what you want."

"Leave her at that? What, as a widow? She gets a hare for an heir? Or they want to get her out of their hair? Or does she become someone's mistress?"

"No, it's a different word," Maury said. "I thought you said *leveret*, *l-e-v-e-r-e-t*. Which is a small hare. It comes from Old French, and ultimately from Latin *lepus*, 'hare'. But you mean *levirate*" – here he pronounced the first syllable as "lee" again – "which comes from Latin *levir*, 'husband's brother'."

"So I was saying it wrong?"

"No," Maury said, "the way you were saying is also acceptable. But ambiguous."

"So neither word has to do with Levites or French lips," Elisa said. (French for 'lips' is *lèvres*.) "Or lovers. But I'm still confused. They practise the brother-in-law?"

"A widow marries her husband's brother. This is actually in Mosaic law, in Deuteronomy: if a man dies before his wife has a child, she has to marry the man's brother to have a child with him. But there is an escape clause: they can renounce the right to marry and the woman is free to marry someone else. Obviously the latter is the norm today, where that law is observed at all. It alleviates the lover-and-levirate problem."

"It's like the brother is the reliever," Elisa said. "So these people in New Guinea are Jewish? Talk about lost tribes."

"No. Other cultures also do it."

174

Elisa sounded out the word silently. "It's a nice word, anyway. Even if a bit pretentious to use it without defining it."

"It's a *lovely* word, I'm sure," Maury said. "C'est la vérité. At least as long as it's more about love than leverage."

"I wonder what the ceremony would be…" Elisa said, canting her eyes up toward the ceiling in thought. "'I hare-by take you, Elvira, as my in-law-fully wedded wife.'" She tittered.

dweeb

WE WERE MILLING AROUND before the official start of the monthly Words, Wines, and Whatever tasting at the Domus Logogustationis, warming up our palates with start-up glasses of wine and some conversation. Arlene was talking about a recent conference she had been to.

"So there was this word challenge thing," Arlene said, "and one of the challenges was that there are only three words in the English language that start with *dw*, and all of them are common words."

I cocked my head slightly and raised an eyebrow. "Three?"

Daryl pulled out his iPad. Arlene darted a hand to block it. "No cheating."

"There must be more than three," I said. "Let's see…"

"No," Arlene said, "let iPad Boy here see if he can cough them up straight out of his cortex without an index."

Darryl pulled a little face. "Um. *Dwell.* Uh, personal names should count – *Dwight, Dwayne…* Oh, *dwindle.* And *dwarf.* Which is actually a noun and a verb, so you can count that twice. We're already over three that way. And *dwelling*! The noun means something not exactly the same as the gerund of the verb. I think that's a pretty comprehensive confutation of the contention." He smiled.

"Dweeb," Arlene said.

"I don't think you're being fair," Daryl said. "Geek, sure, nerd, maybe, but I'm not a dweeb."

"You're not exhaustive, either," Arlene said. "You missed *dweeb.*"

Daryl facepalmed.

Arlene smiled. "I got them all and then I tweeted it." She took a sip of her wine. "Sweet."

"No need to gloat," Daryl said, and turned his attention to his own glass.

"No, this wine is sweet," Arlene said.

"Kabinett," I said. "Riesling." I mused aloud: "*Sweet – tweet – dweeb*…"

"It doesn't really have that much in common with the other *dw* words, does it?" Arlene said. "More with some other words that have that vowel."

Daryl had his iPad in action now. "First *OED* cite is 1982. Which sounds rightish to me. …Probaby comes from *feeb*, for *feeble*, with that *dw* added at the beginning. Maybe from *dwarf*."

"I bet there are some phonaesthetics at work there," I said. "We know that those high front vowels tend to be associated with lighter, smaller, less substantial things. Compare *dweeb* with what it would be if it were, say, *dwab*."

"Sounds like *twat*," Daryl said. "And a twat is more obnoxious and less ineffectual than a dweeb."

"I think the rounded glide into it adds contrast," I added. "Compare *deeb*. Think about how we talk about a tweet rather than a teet."

"Will you stop with the female body parts," Arlene said.

"No, not – oh, never mind," I said. "Anyway, what other words do we get a taste of in *dweeb*?"

"Well, *twee*," Arlene said. "And *wee*."

"And maybe *queen* and *queer*," Daryl said.

"*Oui*," I affirmed. "It's a little farther afield to *squeal*, but then there are those toys, *Weebles*. And *weenie*."

Arlene wagged her finger: "Body parts!" I rolled my eyes.

"*Weed*," Daryl said. "And *Guido*."

"Ooh! *Guido*!" Arlene said. "Is a Guido a dweeb? They're kind of different, aren't they?"

"A dweeb is like a nerd or a geek," Daryl said, "but with excessive self-estimation, combined with a neediness and overearnestness."

"Overweening," I said. "Sort of like a twerp. Which is also a very similar word."

"Ah, yes," said Arlene. "I'll have to tell my tweeps."

"But, by the way," Daryl said, scrolling on his iPad, "there are some other *dw* words that aren't so common: *dwale*, 'deadly nightshade'; *dwalm*, 'swoon'; *dwang*, 'a short piece of reinforcing timber'; *dwerg*, a pseudo-archaic form of 'dwarf'; *dwile*, 'floor-cloth'; *dwine*, 'waste away'; and a bunch of obsolete ones."

"And *dwapp*," Arlene said.

"*Dwapp?*" said Daryl. "That's not in the *OED*."

"As in *Tony Orloongoo and Dwapp*, a fake African music duo from a Don Martin comic strip in *MAD Magazine*?" I said.

"As in *dwapp!*" Arlene said, backhanding Daryl lightly on the side of the head. She turned to me and backhanded me as well. "Dwapp!"

"I think I shall dwalm," Daryl said. "And dwine."

"And whine quite a lot," Arlene said. Then, with a smirk, she said, "Don't dwell on it... dweeb." She tossed back her glass, turned, and went to refill it.

gecko, get-go

MONTGOMERY STARLING-BYRD WAS BACK in town on yet another global word-tasting expedition. A few of us joined him for dinner and drinks. He happened to be seated next to Elisa Lively, and I canted an ear to their conversation. Which did not disappoint.

"Well, we ran into trouble right from the get-go," Elisa was saying.

"From the gecko?" Montgomery said.

"No, from the dog. It kept taking the food."

"From the gecko," Montgomery said, seeking clarification.

"Yes, right from the get-go. It liked lizard food right away."

"As long as it didn't like lizard *for* food."

"Oh," Elisa said, "that's a whole other tale."

"Another tail from the gecko?"

"No, that came later."

"Where was the tail from?"

"From the gecko, but later. Not from the get-go."

"I'm afraid I've lost the thread of the tale here," Montgomery said.

"Well, the gecko's tail was threatened. Actually the dog pulled on it and wouldn't let go, and the gecko dropped it."

"Autotomy," Montgomery observed (that's the word for when a lizard drops its tail).

"It wanted its autonomy, yes. So that was the end of the tail."

"And there was no more."

"No," Elisa said, "it grew another one. Geckos do that."

"Indeed they do. It's a kind of insurance."

I just about choked on my wine stifling a giggle at the thought of the Geico gecko and its accent, which is not quite as plummy as Montgomery's.

"That happened more than once," Elisa said. "But the worst was the noise."

"From the gecko?"

179

"Yes, from the very start. Especially from the dog."

"Why?"

"It didn't like the noise the gecko made."

"Ah, yes: 'Gecko!' That's how they got their name. It's from Malay."

"The poet?"

"What?"

"'I burn the candle at both ends...' She named the gecko?"

"The... Oh, no, the Malay language. In Malaysia. Not Edna St. Vincent Millay."

"Oh. Well," Elisa giggled, "that gecko burned at both ends. It made a noise the dog hated. And so the dog barked like crazy. And the gecko made more noise."

"A sort of gecko echo."

"Yeah! And at the other end there was that tale."

"The end of the tale."

"Repeatedly."

"From the gecko."

"No, not from the get-go."

"From the dog?" Montgomery furrowed his brow.

"No, from the gecko."

"Are you insane, or am I?" Montgomery said, staring abruptly into his wine glass.

I intervened. "Montgomery! Do you mean to say you are unfamiliar with the Americanism – and Canadianism – *from the get-go*?" I pronounced it slowly and clearly.

"From the... *get*? *go*?" Montgomery said. "Oh yes, I see. Voice and place assimilation with reduction: the /t/ devoices the /g/ after it, but also moves to the back and simply pre-stops the stop. Well, this is a very hockey-sounding term. Or perhaps NASCAR. So I take it that it comes from *get going*, which has been shortened and treated as a noun."

"Truncated and mutated," I said.

"Like my gecko," Elisa said.

"I don't think I would," Montgomery said. "I would as soon have a grackle."

"I guess your kind of bird is the starling." Elisa giggled.

"Rather. I prefer a murmuration to the noise of a gecko."

"So would Lawrence," Elisa said.

"Who is Lawrence?"

"My dog."

"Oh," Montgomery said. "And what, dare I ask, was the gecko's name?"

Elisa held her hands wide, palms up, as if to say it was obvious. "Gordon, of course!"

get

It was just after Montgomery's and Elisa's discussion of *get-go* and *gecko* that things almost came to blows.

Not between Elisa and Montgomery, to be sure; rather, the issue was with a prospective member who had joined us at the restaurant, a rather self-important specimen named Will Knott. He caught the end of the discussion on *get-go* and commented, to no one in particular, "I had thought that this was a society for people who valued the English language and knew how to use it well."

"It is for people who love the language and wish to handle its words as fine ingredients in excellent dishes," Montgomery said.

"So how did this one become a member?" he said, jerking his thumb at Elisa. "That's not very good English. *Get-go*." Elisa looked hurt and focused her attention on her wine glass and its emptying and refilling.

"You need to be sensitive to context," I said, my hair starting to stand up on the back of my neck. "I'm not quite sure you got it. It was a colloquial recounting."

He waved me off with his hand before I was done speaking and turned to Montgomery. "I suppose everyone enjoys a bit of slumming now and then, but I certainly wouldn't allow such common – almost vulgar – words in my workplace. I handle important documents."

Montgomery's left eyebrow was arching ever so slightly higher and higher. "Vulgar?"

"*Get. Got.* That's not good English."

"*Get* is not good English?!" I exclaimed, almost disbelieving (I say "almost" because I have once or twice heard of others having the same view).

Will Knott sighed slightly and looked upwards for a moment. Then he continued speaking to Montgomery. "It's a bit discouraging that you have members who are surprised to hear this."

182

"Perhaps," Montgomery said, "it's that they wonder at your placing yourself above Shakespeare, Pope, Dickens, Thackeray, Emerson…"

"Shakespeare had terrible grammar," Will Knott said. "Everyone knows that. Many supposedly great authors were sloppy with their usage."

"You don't like 'Get thee to a nunnery'?"

"He was just trying to fit his meter. He could have said 'Take thou holy orders' or 'Enter the novitiate' or any of several better options. It doesn't even make sense as it is. *Get* means 'receive'. Receive thee to a nunnery?"

"*Get* has a rather broader range of use than that," Montgomery said.

"I'm talking about the proper definition," Will said.

"I thought you said it wasn't a proper word," I said. Will made an eye roll worthy of a fourteen-year-old girl and returned to ignoring me.

"The Germanic root it comes from," Montgomery said, "is one referring to seizing, taking hold of, grasping, obtaining, and such like. The word *get* has, of course, been in the English language as long as there has been an English language to be in."

"A weak defence," Will said. "There are always better words, just as with many other old Anglo-Saxon words. I hope you grasp my meaning. Not get, grasp."

"I don't know that you can always get away with such substitutions," Montgomery said.

"Would you use that sentence in a government report?" said Will. "It would be better as 'Such substitutions may not always be allowed.' Or, to avoid the passive, 'You may not always succeed in making such substitutions.'"

"They don't mean the same thing," I said.

"Could you be quiet?" Will said. "The adults are speaking."

"Get over yourself," I said.

He gave me a condescending look over the tops of his glasses. "*Be less impressed with yourself.*"

"You might want to try to get along with others," Montgomery said.

"*Agree* is a better word than *get along with*," Will replied.

Elisa broke her silence. "Even I know that those don't mean the same thing."

"You do not know all the meanings of the word *agree*," Will said.

"*You* don't know all the meanings of the word *get*," I said. "And you get your back up too readily."

"I am too readily irritated, you mean," he said. "However, it seems to me that you are the one with a temper here."

Montgomery gestured towards me and Elisa. "It is from members such as these that you must get permission to get into the Order of Logogustation."

"Obtain permission," Will said. "*Obtain* is a much better word. And *join* or *enter*, not *get into*."

"You truly feel that this is the way to get ahead?"

"To advance, I believe you mean?"

Montgomery paused and glanced at his watch. "Well, it's getting on."

"The hour is advancing," Will corrected him.

"Let's get this over with," Montgomery said, glancing at me.

"Draw it to a conclusion," Will said.

"Get up," Montgomery said.

"Arise," Will said.

"And get out," Montgomery said.

"Leave, exit, depart," Will said.

"I mean you," Montgomery said. "Do you get it now?"

"Understand it, you mean," Will said.

"We mean get out," I said, positioning myself behind him with two of the waiters, whom I had signalled to come over. "You will never get in. You need to get a clue."

"The door is this way, sir," said one of the waiters. "Don't make us exert ourselves."

Will Knott looked at us distastefully and drew himself up to standing. He looked for moment more and made a bee-line for the door, muttering "Disappointing!" loudly enough for all to hear.

"You ignorant git," I said after him as he left, exited, departed.

mortadella

"WHAT'S THIS?" EDGAR FRICK held up a pink cube of some kind of comestible.

His better half, Marilyn, glanced over. "I'm pink, therefore I'm ham."

Maury, who – as often – was bustling about setting up the food for this month's Words, Wines, and Whatever tasting, stopped long enough to say "Mortadella." Then he continued setting foodstuffs out.

"Baloney," Edgar said, and popped it into his mouth.

"Not exactly," said Maury over his shoulder as he bustled about. "Bologna – or baloney – is an American version of mortadella, but this is the real thing. From Bologna. The city."

"No," said Edgar, "mortadella is a great big pink slice. Like this." He gestured with his hands. "In fact, an end of a mortadella looks pretty much like –" he reached over towards his better half, in partic-ular a rounder part of her anatomy, but she swatted his hand away. "Hm!" he said. "Cruella!"

"It'll be the morta della you," she said, more leering than indig-nant. Then, to Maury, "Isn't that what *mortadella* means? 'Death of the'? Death of the what? Do they know?" She looked skeptically at the white stuff dotting the pink mass.

"That would be *morte della*," I volunteered. "Or *morte dello*, or *del*, or *delle*, or *degli*, or *dei*."

"Well, I'm still wondering what fell into the sausage grinder," she said, impaling the cube on an inch-long vampire-red little fingernail. She waggled it at Edgar and then ate it as though she were doing a community theatre version of *Tom Jones*.

"The white lumps are pork fat," Maury said from partway across the room. "It is also seasoned with black pepper and myrtle."

"Myrtle!" Marilyn exclaimed. "That was my aunt's name. I always wondered what happened to her…"

"So it's myrtle-della," Edgar said, and found it not beneath him to eat another cube.

Maury's orbit drew him nearer again. "It's thought that the name *mortadella* comes from Latin *murtatum*, meaning 'seasoned with myrtle berries', and a diminutive ending *ella*."

"Ella was my other aunt," Marilyn said. "Her ending was not diminutive. If you think mine is something to see…" She edged her leather-cased rotund end towards Maury, who quickly jumped over to the next table.

"Perhaps this is *morte di Ella*," I suggested, spearing a cube with a toothpick.

"It has also, on the other hand," Maury said, "been long held that the name comes from *mortaio*, referring to the mortar in which the meat was pounded."

Marilyn cocked her head at Maury and raised a leering eyebrow. Maury sighed, realizing his unintended double entendre, and drew further away.

"It's a big-sounding word," I said, trying unsuccessfully to divert the conversation from its downward trend. "I mean, four syllables, that rather big back round effect on 'mort', uh… *Della* could be a name of someone big, though it could also be small…"

"But really," Edgar said, eating yet another cube, "mort a deli ever serve it this way?"

"In the orbit of Bologna," Maury said, trying to remain in the conversation without getting too close to Marilyn's centre of gravity, "it is often served this way at the beginning of a meal, with rustic bread."

"So where's the bread?" I asked.

"I was just about to bring it out," he said.

Marilyn stepped forward and reached her hands towards Maury, rolling the fingers in the air in her best vampirella fashion. Impaled on her nails were the last ten cubes of the mortadella. "Just bring your buns here, dear boy," she purred.

Maury stepped back. "You will be the death of me," he croaked, and disappeared into the kitchen.

Marilyn shrugged and proffered her digits to me and Edgar. "Finger food?"

crispy

"How would you like your bacon?" Maury asked, leaning into the dining area from his kitchen. "Crisp?"

Arlene nodded.

"Crispy," Jess answered.

Maury raised an eyebrow and retreated. Arlene smiled with approval: "Not just crisp. Crispy!"

"Aren't they the same thing, though?" Daryl said, pursing his lips.

"Well," I said, "easy to check." Daryl had already gotten out his iPad and was doing some looking up, but that wasn't what I had in mind. "Try swapping in one for the other."

"'They have chicken fingers,'" Arlene said, quoting an ad that was on TV a lot a couple of years ago. "'*Crisp* ones.' Oh, yes, not quite the same. Too technical. Not playful."

"The diminutive effect of the suffix," Jess said. "Sort of like the difference between a *thing* and a *thingy*."

"Funny," Arlene said. "If I talk about something as being *orangey*, it's just orange-ish. Or a *greeny-blue* – more of a tendency. But *crispy* isn't just *crispish*."

"But try substituting the other way," I said. "How's the weather outside? In January it can be crisp. But when is it crispy?"

"Arizona in July," Daryl said.

"Heat! It connotes overcooking!" Arlene said.

"If someone gives you a crisp retort…" Jess said.

"Icy," Arlene said. "But if it's crispy… ooh, *tsszt*" (she made as if touching something hot).

"Crisp consonants can be good for singing," I said. "Crispy ones, not so much perhaps. Sounds kind of crunchy almost. And I like nice, crisp definition in a picture. I have no idea what crispy definition might be. Maybe over-sharpened."

"I like a nice, crisp shirt," Arlene said. "A crispy shirt sounds like high fashion. Or clubwear."

"Maybe you've just gotten a little crispy," Daryl said, miming smoking marijuana. I glimpsed Urban Dictionary on his iPad. "But crispy is a good thing if you're going out. 'You look crispy.' Stylish, smart, confident. Not crepitating but scintillating."

"And apparently with freshly curled hair," Jess said.

"Crispy curls?" Arlene said.

"*Crispus*. Latin for 'curly,'" Jess explained.

"Know when *crispy* was first used?" Daryl said, looking at his iPad.

"1300-something, wasn't it?" I said.

"Yeah," he said. "1398. That -*y* suffix usually attaches to nouns, but there was a little vogue for extending one-syllable adjectives with it. ... Hm!" He smiled a little. "The *OED* says that this started in the 15th century, if not earlier. Well, 1398 is slightly earlier…"

"You'll have to email Jesse Sheidlower," I said. (He's Editor at Large of the OED.) "He'll probably say, 'Yeah, I know.'"

Maury reappeared from the kitchen carrying plates of brunch, the first two for the ladies. "Crisp," he said, setting a plate in front of Arlene with curly bacon on it. "And crispy," he said, setting down Jess's plate with just a little rap so that the bacon on it shattered.

"Crispy?" Jess said. "Frangible!"

"Friable," I said.

"*Over*-fry-able," Arlene said.

"Buon appetito," Maury said crisply, and returned to the kitchen.

beefcake

"THESE ARE A BIT UNUSUAL for hors d'œuvres," Jess said, looking at the plate Maury had just set down.

"Beefcake," Maury said.

Jess raised an eyebrow. "Looks like meatloaf to me. Quartered slices of meatloaf."

"It's a cake made of beef," Maury said. "Pâté de campagne. A bit of a terrine, even: you will find whole pieces of beef, plus prunes and almonds, and the whole macerated in Armagnac."

"It's not dessert," Jess said.

"Your unfailing eye has… not failed you," Maury said. "That would be cheesecake."

"I could take a bit of cheesecake," Jess mused.

"So could I," said Daryl, who had gravitated to the food. "It's kind of early for that, though. First the hors d'œuvres, then the word and wine tasting, then dessert." He looked around at the other members of the Order of Logogustation slowly gathering for the monthly event. Then he picked up a piece of Maury's offering. "This is what, again?"

"Beefcake," I said.

"Doesn't look like Chippendale dancers," Daryl said. He bit into it. "Hm. It's got a piece of beefsteak in it, though. Maybe it was a mis-steak?"

"Not all cakes are sweet," Maury said.

"Not all beefcakes are male," I said.

"Oh, come on," Jess said. "Female beefcake? Now, I *would* like to see *that*."

"Well, you should go see Cirque du Soleil's *Amaluna*," I said. "There are some very stacked, muscular female gymnasts. My wife called them *beefcake*."

"Why doesn't your wife ever come to these word events?" Daryl asked, while chewing (how uncouth).

"She thinks you're all figments of my imagination," I said.

"I think a female usage of *beefcake* may be a figment of hers," Jess said.

"Oh, no," Maury said, "I've dated one or two women who could fit that definition."

"Am I right," Daryl said, "that *beefcake* is modelled on *cheesecake*, as in an alluringly presented female physique?"

"That seems to be the consensus," I said. "*Cheesecake* was in use by the 1930s to refer to pin-up pictures of pretty women with much exposed flesh. I don't know whether it was meant to make a direct equivalence between the pale thighs and the pale cheesecake, or whether it was just the standard connection between sex and food. *Beefcake* came around by the late 1940s, referring to bare-chest poses of hunky men."

"As opposed to *meatloaf*," Jess said, "which would be chunky men. Like the singer."

"Beefcake men are beefy," I said. "Whereas cheesecake women are not normally called *cheesy*. I think the sound of *beefcake* is a bit more suited to its object: percussive. 'Biff!'" I picked up a piece. "I wonder if you could get something like this in Bishkek."

"More likely than a cheesesteak, I suppose," Maury said. "Although I am not much familiar with Kyrgyz cuisine."

"Say," Jess said, picking up a piece, "didn't you have a little date last night?" She bit in.

Maury paused, pursed his lips. "Yes, this was made for that. Someone I had encountered online. I thought we were going to meet and have a picnic. She said she would bring the cheesecake if I brought the beefcake."

Jess swallowed. "Well, what happened?"

"At the appointed time and place, she arrived, dressed very lightly and not apparently carrying food. I set down my offering. She looked at it and me and said, 'Beefcake? Looks like meatloaf to me.' And deserted."

"Well, we get our just deserts, too, even if it's not dessert," Jess said. "It *is* yummy."

hyperforeignism

ELISA LIVELY HAD INVITED a "well-known world traveller" named Harley Weldon to our monthly Words, Wines, and Whatever tasting event at the Order of Logogustation's headquarters, Domus Logogustationis. "He'll regale you with stories," she promised.

And she was right. He had a story for everything. He held forth in his spot at our table. (Jess, I, and Maury held first, second, and third, respectively; Elisa held fifth.)

"I remember," he said, with a practiced misty, thoughtful look, to his glass of Bordeaux, "drinking a claret much like this in Beijing. The restaurant had matched it with a dish that, to my surprise, contained prodigious quantities of habanero peppers. I almost thought it was an empanada."

I held up four fingers under the table in sight of Jess and Maury. Jess smirked. We had been keeping score, you see.

Oh, yes, you can't see on paper what we were keeping score of. His actual pronunciation was "a cla-ray much like this in bay-zhing," "prodigious quantities of ha-ba-nye-ro peppers," and "em-pan-ya-da." That's four goofs:

1. *Claret* is properly pronounced like the last two syllables of "declare it"; it's an English word based on the French word *clairet*, which means something else.

2. The closest you'll get with English phonotactics to the Chinese pronunciation of *Beijing* is "bey-jing," with an English-style "j" and not a "zh" as in *beige*.

3. *Habanero* is not *habañero*. It is an adjective formed on *Havana* – in Spanish, *v* and *b* have a certain interchangeability – and there is no palatalization of the *n*. Also, the *h* is not pronounced in Spanish – though it has come to be pronounced in the English version.

4. *Empanada* is likewise not *empañada*. The latter word actually means 'fogged up'. Sort of like his pronunciation.

Our hyperactive foreign traveller, in other words, was proving to be a high-performance source of hyperforeignisms: overcorrecting for difference from English – matching a word to a conjectural "foreign" pronunciation pattern not appropriate to it. The word *hyperforeignism* is a simple English confection of the Greek-derived *hyper* and the Latin-derived *ism* with the word *foreign*, which came from Latin *foris* "outside" by way of French *forain*, plus a hypercorrecting addition of a *g* to match words such as *reign* and *sign*.

"That was quite a coup de grâce to our tête-à-tête," he said, as "coo de graw" and "teh a teh"; Elisa listened, rapt, while Maury, Jess, and I tried not to choke on our beverages. Drop the end of *coup de grâce* and it sounds like *coup de gras*, meaning 'stroke of fat'. Amazing how often one hears people dropping *all* consonants at the ends of French words, even when there's an *e* after them. As if to prove the point, he added, "I could have killed for some Vichyssoise." Yes, he said it as "vishy-swa."

"I'm no stranger to strong flavours, of course," he went on. "One time dining with a Punjabi chap near the Taj Mahal I had some Earl Grey with a stunning excess of bergamot. I felt like a cross between Kahlil Gibran and Genghis Khan." A flurry of fingers up under the table: one for "poon-jobby" rather than "pun-jobby" (the *u* is to approximate a more central vowel, like English "uh," in the older British way of transliterating by English spelling habits rather than by consistent phonemics); one for "tazh" rather than "taj" (again like *Beijing*: there's this idea many people have that *j* couldn't possibly be like our English "j" sound in any other language); one for dropping the "t" on the end of *bergamot* (it's not a French word – French for it is *bergamotte* – and it's not from the Italian city of Bergamo); and one each for hard "g" in *Gibran* and *Genghis* (nearly everyone gets those wrong these days; those names were given English spellings back when "j" before *e* or *i* was spelled with a *g* by habit in English versions. You could protest that by now the usage has changed and it's no longer wrong in English, just as we say, for instance, *Paris* like an English word; but if you want to get it true to the original – and the intent of the English spelling, which ironically is what's misleading us – you would do better with the "j").

"But I'd still take that over the time I had tea with some Russian mafiya men in a dacha near St. Petersburg." Two fingers: he said "ma-*fee*-ya" – actually *mafiya* is just an English transliteration of the Russian transliteration of the Italian word *mafia*, which is pronounced in Russian as in Italian with the stress on the first syllable – and "dakha" rather than with the *ch* like English "ch." Again: the idea that *ch* couldn't possibly be said like English *ch* in any other language.

"*That* was like a scene from Brueghel." I flipped up another finger and tried not to roll my eyes: "broigl." (*Brueghel*, sometimes spelled *Breughel* or *Bruegel*, is a Dutch name, and the *ue* or *eu* is like French *eu* – and the *g* or *gh* is, in Dutch, like a voiced "kh," but you don't need to do that in English, which no longer has that sound.)

"A festival of machismo," he added. Another finger: he had made the *ch* in *machismo* into a "k."

"Quite the opposite of that time in Reykjavik, when I was listening to Berlioz with some Japanese-Icelandic friends – did you know they existed? Not even immigrants; nissei or sansei." Man, this guy was a treat, and he was now overapplying the German pronunciation of *ei* (like English "eye"): "rye-kya-vik" rather than "rey"; "niss-eye" and "san-sigh" instead of "nee-say" and "san-say." Also he dropped the *z* on *Berlioz*.

Harley finished his glass of Bordeaux and reached for some of the sausage and cured meat on the table. He looked up and around the room, trying to spot something.

"Do you need help locating anything?" Maury asked.

Harley pointed at a table halfway across the room. "I'll be right back. I just want to get some Riesling to go with the prosciutto and chorizo." He stepped away quickly enough that he probably didn't notice when Jess, Maury, and I all burst into giggles and held up three fingers each: one for "rise-ling" instead of "reez-ling," one for "pros-choo-toe" instead of "pro-shoo-toe" (in Italian, the "t" is double, like in English *coattail*, but in English we generally don't manage that), and one for "core-eed-zo" instead of "cho-ree-so."

"If he had just managed the 'ch' in the right meat, that would have been a start," Jess said, and tossed back the last of her claret. "But I do hope he brings the bottle. I need some."

Elisa looked a little confused. "So… what do you all think of Harley Weldon?"

"Oh, his travelogues are most diverting," Maury said. "He's learned all sorts of interesting things around the world."

"Surprisingly enough," I said, "not including much of anything about other languages."

"But he used all sorts of non-English words!" Elisa said.

"True, true," I said. "But I wouldn't say his pronunciation is well-done."

Jess nodded and giggled some more. "Harley." Or was that "Hardly"?

incent, incentivize

"I'm incensed!"

Margot swatted a small sheaf of papers down on the table, nearly toppling our paper coffee cups. Of course, if anyone would edit on paper, it would be Margot, age 30-going-on-80.

I raised an eyebrow. "What has you burning up?"

Jess, at the same time, said about the same thing: "What's the incendiary device?"

"Look!" Margot thrust the top page forward and jabbed her finger at a line. We craned forward, Jess, Daryl, and I, trying to read it. Margot, after hesitation, read it out loud to prevent knocking of heads. "'We have season's tickets to Maple Leafs games, but client demand for these seats is less than formerly. We have previously had raffles to give away game tickets to employees. We have decided to incentivize these seats. One pair will be given to a top performer every two weeks to incent our employee population.'"

I clucked my tongue. "Yeah, needs a little work. Amazing that they asked, though. This kind of stuff usually goes out as is."

Jess sat back. "I'm not surprised that client demand for Leafs tickets is down." She knew, as I did, that the very usage *Leafs* irritated Margot, but as a brand name it's regularized – *maple leaves* are actual foliage.

"Yeah," said Daryl, stepping in the biggest cow patty, "that's not how one usually uses *incentivize*."

Margot's eyes swivelled onto him like two overloading lasers. "One does not. Use. *Incentivize*. At all. Ever."

"Well, I don't see why one would need to," I said, trying to keep a straight face. "When there's a perfectly good word already. *Incent*." I tried to have a sip of my coffee without giggling.

Margot looked at me for a moment as though she was going to say "You stay out of this," and then remembered it wasn't a lovers' spat between her and Daryl. Finally she said, "That is a perfectly awful word."

"It's a perfectly elegant word," I said, the corner of my mouth curling up. "A tidy backformation from *incentive*. Been around since the mid-1800s. Whereas *incentivize* showed up in the 1960s." Daryl, meanwhile, was tapping away on his iPad.

"What's wrong with *give an incentive*?" Margot said.

"It's three words where one will do?" I said.

"To be fair," Jess said, sitting forward again, "those older uses of *incent* are with the older sense. They mean 'incite'."

"Sure," I said, "because *incentive* meant 'incitement' – the current sense of 'reward' or 'encouragement' didn't show up until the mid-1900s. *Incent* was a backformation from the older sense, and now it's one from the newer sense."

Daryl laughed at something on his iPad. "On Merriam-Webster, they have comment threads –"

Margot and Jess simultaneously exclaimed, with entirely different tones, "On a dictionary?!"

"Yeah! And the top comment on their entry for *incent* is, 'I am shocked this is in a dictionary. I hear "incent" all the time at work and I just don't think it's a real word. Nor have I any use for "incentivize". That's even worse.'" Daryl laughed again as he looked up. "Usually prescriptivists refer to a dictionary to prove something's 'not a word.' Now this guy finds *incent* in the dictionary and he won't accept its authority."

Jess intoned a chant: "'It's not a word, it's not a word...' The old familiar incantation."

I looked at her for a moment. "You know, don't you."

"...That *incentive* and *incantation* have the same Latin root? Why yes, I do." Jess smiled broadly. "*Canere*, to sing. Incentives set the tune. Well, now they not so much call the tune as pay the piper."

"Same person," Daryl said. "Calls the tune, pays the piper."

"Formerly," I said, "*incentive* was sometimes mistakenly thought to have the same root as *incense*, verb and noun, which is actually the same as *incendiary* – since an incentive gets people all fired up."

"Well," Jess said, "*incent* seems to make cense." She sipped her coffee and glanced at me, evidently confident that I would hear the pun she meant – with the old cut-off version of *incense*.

"It makes nonsense," Margot said. She looked as if someone had just put lemon juice in her coffee.

"You know what it means," I said. "You just don't like it because it's business-speak."

"What if we always backformed words like that?" Margot said. "If instead of sending someone a missive we said we missed them?"

"If I miss you, I'll send you a missive," Daryl said. "To say so."

Margot froze for a moment and then continued. "And instead of giving a laxative we laxate?"

"I think we could laxate this document of yours," Jess said, reaching for it.

"Ugghhhh," Margot said, reacting to the document, Jess's use of *laxate*, or both.

"Yeah, never mind whether those are real words," I said, "it's a bit of a piece of sh–"

"Ssshhh!" Margot said. She's allergic to crude words. She gathered up the document. "I can handle this. I wasn't looking for help. I simply wanted to air my frustration."

Jess and I looked at each other. Why she would air it in our direction was an ongoing mystery. She couldn't possibly be expecting simple sympathy.

Daryl set aside his iPad. "What incentive are you getting for editing this?"

"Tickets to the Maple –" Margot hesitated. "The…" Could she make herself say *Leafs*? She exhaled through her nose. "To a hockey game."

Jess rolled her head over to face Margot. "The Leafs? I wouldn't be incented. I'd be incensed."

at the end of the day

"AT THE END OF THE DAY," the guy with the orange polyster tie said, "we're all about value here. Value and quality."

Maury looked skeptical. This was his first time buying a new car (after all these years), but he had heard stories. "Does it get good gas mileage? All things considered?"

"Well, you know, you drive some in the city, you drive some in the country, but a car you get from us, at the end of the day, it's going to be economical with the gas." He leaned his torso in its checked jacket against a counter and took a slug of his coffee.

"What is the service record like, in the long run?"

"I'm telling you, at the end of the day, the cars we sell have better service records than any other make." He paused, then nodded once for emphasis.

"And yet you're selling the extra protection warranty. In the final analysis, is that such a good deal, then?" Maury circled the car one more time, running his finger along the detailing.

"You know, if it were just you and the car…" The salesman made a flat wipe with his hand. "You wouldn't need it. But there are other drivers out there, and nature. Rocks. Ice. At the end of the day, that warranty is a good deal."

Maury raised an eyebrow and he and I exchanged a glance. This salesman sure was focused on the end of the day. I was wondering if he was impatient to go home. I glanced at the clock: still just early afternoon. Well, people do tend to speak in habitual manners, and fads come and go for clichés. *At the end of the day* has been in use in its figurative sense at least since the 1970s – but it didn't take long for the *Oxford English Dictionary* to include "hackneyed" as part of its definition.

"The handling in difficult conditions?" Maury asked. He opened the driver's door and sat on the side of the seat.

"At the end of the day," salesdude said, one arm holding coffee cup leaning against the door frame, "any car you get from us will handle better than any other one you can get."

"So, in sum, all in all, when all is said and done…" Maury said.

"At the end of the day?"

"Sub specie aeternitatis?" Maury said. The salesman looked at him blankly. "When it comes down to it, is it really the best one *for me*? Or should I look at a few more?"

"At the end of the day, you won't find another car that's better for your needs."

"And are you really, when it's all added up, giving me the best deal you can? Are there other plans, other promotions, other incentives –"

"At the end of the day, no." Salesmeister swept his hands apart smartly. "You won't come out further ahead than what I'm offering you."

Maury paused a moment. "Very well, then…"

I didn't think I could trust the salesman as far as I could throw him. But Maury clearly liked the car, and he was just seeking assurances. The salesman seemed confident and forthright enough to him.

Looking back, though, one thing is clear to us: Maury should have come back in the evening, just before closing. The car Maury bought that afternoon turned out to be a lemon and an open sore on his bank account. Everything the salesman said may have been true… but we'll never know, because it wasn't the end of the day.

urban, urbane

It was an early warm day and Maury and I were sitting on a patio having a beverage (one each, actually). I had just answered a question for Maury when I heard a familiar British accent say, "Who said *urban?*"

It was Marcus Brattle, my mentee, now 16 years old and devoted as ever to hip-hop. He had rolled up on a skateboard, no mean feat with his pants around his ankles.

"Well," I said, looking from young Marcus to the rather more seasoned Maury, "here is a study in the difference a letter can make." I paused for effect. I gestured to Marcus. "Urban." I turned to Maury. "Urbane."

"We're all urban," Maury pointed out. "We all live in the city."

"True," I said, "and while I love the fresh air of the country and a nice walk among the trees, I don't mind not having to say *rural* all the time. The same 'rrr' as in *urban* but with more of the same. I like the nice 'bun' of *urban*. But –" I turned again towards Marcus – "Marcus here likes what is often called *urban music*. Even though it is much beloved of suburban youths."

"I'm not suburban," Marcus said.

"True dat," I said. "I would have to say Maury's tastes are more urbane, though. Jazz and classical. Everything smoother. Just as *urbane* is *urban* with an *e*, to be urbane is to be urban with ease."

"I might say," Maury said, "that *urbane* is to *urban* as *humane* is to *human*. The *e* word is characteristic of those most positive qualities associated with the non-*e* word."

"And like *humane* from *human*, *urbane* was originally just an alternative version of *urban*," I said. "And of course they're all from Latin."

"Speaking of smooth," Marcus said, "what are you drinking?"

We raised our glasses in unison and said, "Bourbon."

"Not *bourbane?*" Marcus smirked a little at his own witticism. "And why are you sitting outside?"

"Because we can," Maury said.

"Although I would be happy away from the smoke," I said, glancing towards its source at a nearby table. "Say, do you know who instituted the world's first smoking ban?"

Semi-expectant blank looks from both other parties.

"Pope Urban VII," I said. "He threatened to excommunicate anyone who took tobacco in a church or on its porch, whether by chewing, sniffing, or smoking."

"Didn't his papacy last only 13 days?" said Maury.

"True," I said. "Must have been the tobacco lobby."

"So why were you talking about urban anyway?" asked Marcus.

Maury and I looked at each other for a moment, brows furrowed. I blinked a couple of times. Then Maury said, "Japan."

"Ah, yes," I said.

"I guess Japan is urban," Marcus said, "but so is China, so is…"

"Well, and Japan is especially urban in China," I said.

"What?" Marcus gave me a please-make-sense look.

"Mandarin for 'Japan' is pronounced pretty much exactly like *urban*," I said. "That's what I was saying."

Marcus raised one eyebrow. "I'm certain that with that tidbit of information I am well on my way to becoming more urbane." He dropped his skateboard on the ground, swatted my hat off my head and sailed off.

"Ur-bane of my existence," I said, and got up to grab my urban turban.

gastropub

Maury and I decided, for the latest in our occasional beer-and-beer-and-food-and-beer sprees, to try the Cobra and Mongoose. Which is a gastropub.

Which of course came up as we were sitting there, surveying our menus, with our pints of local 8.7% microbrews served in improbable Mason jars.

"This *is* a gastropub," Maury said, arching one eyebrow as he scanned the food list.

"Not a word I much like," I said. I looked up and surveyed the surroundings, a pastiche of British Raj and modern Hounslow references somehow reminiscent of the dining room decor of the Pale Man from *El laberinto del fauno* (misnamed in English as *Pan's Labyrinth*).

"Don't like the air of *gastrointestinal, gastroenteritis, gastroileostomy,* and so on and so on?"

"And *gas*," I said. "It doesn't help that *gastronomy*, the source of the *gastro*, has the stress on the second syllable whereas *gastropub* has it on the first like all those words having to do with medical things and conditions."

"You just can't quite stomach it," Maury said. *Gastro* comes from Greek γαστήρ *gastér* 'stomach'.

"And it somehow makes the *pub*, which by itself is fine, sound like burbles from the belly, or a brief eructation or burst of flatulence," I said.

"I assume you don't mind that it's macaronic," Maury said. By this he meant that it mixes roots from different languages – in this case the *pub* is short for *public house*, and *public* comes from Latin *publicus* by way of French.

"I do not," I said, eyes fixed on my menu, "but I'm not sure whether I mind that it's macaroni."

"Macaroni?" Maury arched an eyebrow. "I see burgers."

We exchanged menus. They had separate menus for starch and meat and had given us one of each. Cute. The third menu, lying on the table, proved to be not wine but vegetables. We left it untouched. The beer list was scrawled in chalk on the wall, with daily specials written in dry-erase marker in stall number 3 of the washroom.

"Everyone is doing burgers," I said, looking at the meat menu. "Oh, look, they also have steak and kidney pie and bangers and mash and all that sort of thing. What's the deal with the *gastro*? This is all pub."

"Fine restaurants are now taking those items onto their menus," Maury said. "So they are gastro. And apparently it has come full circle now. I think I'll have the pancakes."

"What's special about them?"

"They don't say. Except that there's an asterisk. Oh. With foie gras. Hm. I'll try it."

"Oh, look," I said, "Bavarian sausage. Apparently a Gasthaus thing. Which is what a gastropub might have been if they had taken less of *gastronomy* and the other end of *public house*."

A heavy-lidded waiter who evidently went to Medusa's hairdresser arrived to take our order on his iPhone. Maury went with the pancakes. I went with the sausage with a side of chicken-fried fat. By the time we had taken the foam off our third pints, our gastro had arrived.

"Curry," Maury said. I looked at his pancakes. They looked normal and plain. "I believe the griddle is seasoned with it," he explained.

"I remember a restaurant near where I used to work that served curry-flavoured pancakes. Not intentionally." I started into my sausage. "Currywurst," I said. Indeed, there was a dusting of curry powder all over the top of the sauce.

"I thought they said Bavarian," Maury said.

"Currywurst is a Berlin thing, yes, isn't it," I said. "They're all over the map."

We mounted a proper assault on our food with the aid of pints number four. I further polished off 75% of the jar of Major Grey chutney that they had deposited on the table. By the end of the meal my gastrointestinals were burbling.

"Who do we have to thank for this trend?" I said at last.

"It started in Britain in the early '90s," Maury said. "A pub in the London area that decided to start serving acceptable food."

"And still keep that popular pub atmosphere," I said.

"Pub," Maury said. I almost said "What?" but I realized that he was dealing with a gastro issue when he added "Pubbbbbrrrrr."

"Oh dear," I said. "How do your guts feel?"

"Like a cobra and a mongoose getting to know each other," Maury said. Then he raised an eyebrow, raised his index finger, stood up, and sprinted to the W.C.

tenterhooks

"I'LL BUY YOU A COFFEE if you guess what these are," Jess said. She held out a little box.

Daryl looked in. "Bent nails," he said tentatively.

"To a certain extent," Jess said. "But what's their intent?"

"To frustrate carpenters," I said.

"A bit of a stretch," Jess said.

"They're supposed to be like that?" Daryl said.

"It's intentional."

"It would help to see them in context," I said.

"Obviously. Once you have them in the frame, you'll catch on."

"Or they'll catch on," I said. "But catch on what?"

"Feel free to ask around," Jess said. "Canvas."

"Ask strangers here in the coffee shop?" Daryl said.

"Get the answer by hook or by crook."

"They do look like crooked fingers," I said, crooking my index finger.

"There's some tension between form and function."

"Are you going to keep on at this?" Daryl asked. He gazed at the box intently.

"Maybe I'll keep *you* on this. On these."

"On tenterhooks," I said.

Jess smiled and pocketed the box. "What do you take in your coffee?"

"Wait, what?" Daryl said. "He didn't make a guess."

"He got it for all in tents," Jess said.

I smiled and extended a finger. "And on tenters."

"Will you explain!" Daryl said.

"Don't have a tenter tantrum," Jess said. She headed over to the counter.

"A tenter," I said, "is a frame on which canvas or other fabric is stretched to dry. From Latin *tendere* 'stretch', source of assorted other English words, including *tent* and *extend*."

"What will it be?" Jess shouted at me from the counter.

"Decaf, cream," I shouted back.

"But what are those, then?" Daryl said. "Don't hang me out to dry here."

"Before you rack your brain, put your brain to the rack," I said. "A tenter needs hooks. To hold the fabric in place."

The lightbulb went on over Daryl's head. "Tenterhooks."

"It's not a Dutch family name!" I said.

"Not tenderhooks, either," he said.

"Whatever those would be. No, if you feel like you're in a state of tension, stretched and drying, you're on tenterhooks."

"Which would put me in Jess's pocket now," Daryl said.

Jess came back with the coffee. "Better luck next time," she said. "James nailed it."

elute

"For every problem," Maury said, raising his glass, "there is a solution."

"Of, in this case, twelve percent ethanol," I said. I was examining the bottle from which Maury had filled his glass. I did not recognize the winery. The label had a convoluted, tie-dyed-looking design. "Where did you get this?"

"A loot bag," Maury said. "Some conference thing." He swirled the wine and sniffed for a moment and winced slightly.

"When was the last conference you went to?" The label was cagey about the exact year the wine was made.

"Er... a few years ago. I happened on this while cleaning out a closet." He held it up to the light. It appeared opaque.

"That's pretty dark, even for Zinfandel."

"Even for Coca-Cola."

"I wonder if it could elute the rust from a nail." Coke supposedly do that – *elute* means 'remove by dissolution': something is adsorbed (coated) onto something else, an a solvent picks it up and takes it away, or else binds better to the surface and displaces it. From Latin *e* 'away' and *luere*, combining form of *lavere* 'wash'.

"Well..." Maury shrugged. He took a large sip from the glass. For a split second he attempted to swish it in his mouth, but reflex took over and he did a perfect spit take: he blew an aerosol of the wine all over the front of his refrigerator. I stepped back automatically, but by good luck I was out of the spray cone anyway.

"Aghl," Maury said as he emptied his glass into the sink and filled it with water. He swished some water in his mouth and spat it into the sink. And again. He turned to me. "I think that would elute the enamel from my teeth."

"Which conference was it you got this at?"

"Um... that eludes me. It doesn't seem to have been an elite event."

"Well. You found a bottle of wine. At first you were elated, but you turn out to have been deluded." I turned to look at his fridge. "And your refrigerator... may soon be denuded." The wine, as it dripped down the front, appeared to be making streaks in the paint.

"Good grief, it *is* eluting enamel," Maury said. He leaned closer to look, then grabbed a paper towel and started to wipe, which almost seemed to aggravate the damage.

"And epoxy," I said. "Appliance paint."

I looked at the effect on the fridge for a moment, then reached over and held up the wine bottle. "I think I know where they got their label design."

"Cork that and set it someplace safe," Maury said, still wiping. "I'm going to keep it. I'm all out of drain clearing fluid. ...What, by the way, were the tasting notes on the back of the bottle?"

I looked at the bottle. A drip from Maury's pouring of it had made its way down across the back label and obliterated the centre of it. I held it out to him. "I'm afraid it elutes description."

merry

I ARRANGED FOR THE USUAL coffee bunch to meet at Starbucks this time. I did this solely for the enjoyment of provoking Margot with their latest seasonal campaign slogan. I succeeded.

"'Let's merry'? *'Let's merry'?!*" She was frothing more than a cappuccino would.

"You're not merrying," I said. "It's Christmas. Or advent, anyway. You should merry!"

"I'm not the merrying kind," she said with some asperity.

"Don't I know it," said Daryl sotto voce. Margot was momentarily nonplussed and decided to blush.

"It *is* rather odd," Jess said, blowing on her eggnog latte.

"I would have thought you would be defending it," Margot said, regaining her voice. "Your precious verbing and all that. And no doubt there's some historical usage of *merry* as a verb."

"The latter is confirmed," Daryl said, scrolling through the *OED* on his iPad. "Both transitive and intransitive. I merry you, you merry me, let's merry."

"Enough," Margot said in a barely audible whisper, her skin colour increasingly Christmassy – red with shades of green.

Daryl continued, waving his hand at his iPad with an almost studied casualness. "Interestingly, *merry* has a lot of cognates in Indo-European languages, and most of them have something to do with brevity. Indeed, even Latin *brevis* is a related word: there's a predictable transformation between /b/ and /m/ and between /w/ and /g/. It seem that pleasantry and mirth – that's another related word, *mirth* – it seems they make the time pass more quickly."

"Ironically," Jess said, "getting short with people has rather the opposite effect."

"But that's all adjectival originally," I said. "And it's not really in current use as a verb."

"The *OED* has intransitive use into the 20th century," Daryl said. "Latest citation is from James Joyce. It's figurative, mostly. 'Warm sunshine merrying over the sea.' The transitive use is cited up to 1961... Oh, but with *up*: 'merry up their hearts'; 'people merrying-up themselves'..."

"Oh, well that's a bit different," I said. "You can use quite a lot of words with *up* to make causative transitive verbs. 'She prettied up her face and uglied up her attitude,' for example. It's a sort of modular formation. And for the intransitive, as a figurative usage, it's less surprising. Again, 'A warm sunset oranging on the horizon' would not be such an odd figure."

Margot seemed genuinely surprised. "So you really don't like it," she said to me.

"Didn't say that," I said. "I'm just accounting for its seeming odd. We don't verb adjectives of state as much as we do adjectives of activity and nouns, I don't think. Anyway, you're going to have to get used to it."

"It sounds like Chinglish," Margot said. "Or Japlish. Like some packaging or some cheap Xbox game."

"Starbucks say 'All your base are belong to us,'" I said.

"But why not *be merry* or *make merry*?" Margot protested.

"Or even *get merry*," Daryl mused apart as though to no one in particular. "'We got married on Christmas.'" He sipped his caramel brûlé latte and looked at not Margot.

"Would you really go with *be merry*?" I asked Margot, whose lower lip seemed to be shaking slightly. "Don't you tell your English tutoring students to avoid forms of *to be* when they can? There's a certain prejudice against them. Admittedly, many texts can be greatly improved by moving away from *be-* and noun-centred constructions and into action verbs. But sometimes it leads to rather forced results."

"*Make merry* is nice and active," Jess said.

"It's still two words," I said. "There's an idea that one-word verbs are better than compound predicates. Some people absolutely hate adverbs. Most verbs could of course be paraphrased as another verb plus an adverb, and there's no reason in principle that a given verb-adverb combination couldn't be expressed as a one-word verb if one existed. It just happens that many of them don't have single words. And a single word is punchier. It occurs to me that *make* plus adjective, intransitive, tends to show up in phrases referring to intercourse: *make love, make whoopee, makin' bacon...*"

"*Merry*, meanwhile, gets around quite a bit," Daryl said, again with the iPad. "*Merry and bright, merry-faced, merry-hearted, merry-lipped, merry-mouthed, merry-voiced, merry Monday, merry night, merry Christmas. The more the merrier.* Two are merrier than one. 'Tis the season to merry, it seems. So let's! Time's a-wasting."

"Then why make it pass more quickly," Margot said quietly, eyes downward. She stood, pulled her coat around her. "A happy Christmas to you," she said, looking at me and then at Jess. She glanced quickly at Daryl, then turned and hurried towards the door.

"Have a happy," I said. She broke her stride for half a moment, her hands tensing perceptibly, but then passed through the door. I looked back to see Daryl stuffing his iPad in his bag and getting up.

"Gentlemen," he said, nodding at me and Jess. He made towards the door.

Jess raised one eyebrow, and then lifted her cup in a toast towards him. "God rest you married," she said, slightly indistinctly, as he exited.

"Yow know," I said, relaxing back in my chair, "that conversation couldn't have happened quite that way if we had British accents."

"Where *merry* and *marry* are not homophones. Indeed." She looked into her cup and saw residue encircling it. "Oh look. Starbucks has even given me a ring. I guess they really do want to merry."

otiose

"WELL, THAT WAS OTIOSE."

Maury and I had come into a building and taken an elevator up one floor. Then we had walked down the hall and found ourselves taking a ramp back down a half a floor. Meeting it at the level we were heading to was a ramp up a half a floor from where we had gotten on the elevator.

"Odious, in fact," I said.

"But was it Otis?"

"An otiose detail. Any make of elevator would have been equally irrelevant."

Perhaps I should explain *otiose* for those who know it not. It means 'without practical result; futile; pointless'. It comes from Latin *otioisus* 'at leisure, unemployed, ineffectual, inactive, without issue', from *otium* 'leisure, peace, freedom, lack of business'. *Otiose* is a negative term, but *otium* – a word rarely used in English – names something we value.

We walked on. "It's not as though we're in a hurry, mind you," Maury said. "We have plenty of time."

"Ample otium," I said. "The pleasure of leisure."

"Tainted by the odium of the otiose."

Maury stopped walking and looked at me; I stopped because he stopped. "All of this doesn't work," he said, "for those who pronounce it 'o-she-owes' rather than 'o-tee-owes.'"

"Utterly otiose," I said. But I said the *s* as [s], not as [z] like Maury. And yet all the variations are equally acceptable. "Atra-otiose," I said, with the "she" pronunciation (a reference to *atrabilious*). "Atrocious."

We started walking again and arrived shortly at the door we sought. It was closed. It announced the professor's office hours. They did not include the time of our arrival.

"I have an issue with this," I said.

"I find it without issue," Maury parried.

"We should have checked ahead of time."

"Ah, but we did not, and we came afoot, and found it a waist of time."

"Oh, tedious."

We started walking back and came soon to the up-down ramp split.

"Well," Maury said, gesturing towards the upward ramp, "shall we take the elevator down?"

CPSIA information can be obtained
at www.ICGtesting.com
Printed in the USA
BVHW031815291120
594440BV00025B/203